1964

THE NEWS
THE EVENTS
AND
THE LIVES
OF 1964

William Dean
D'Azur Publishing

Published by D'Azur Publishing 2023
D'Azur Publishing is a Division of D'Azur Limited

Copyright © D'Azur Publishing 2023

William Dean has asserted his rights under the Copyright, Design and Patents Act 1988 to be identified as the author of this work.

The language, phrases and terminology within this book are as written at the time of the news reports during the year covered and convey the sentiments at that time. The news reports are taken from internationally recognised major newspapers and other sources of the year in question.
The language does not represent any personal view of the author or publisher.

All Rights Reserved. No part of this publication may be reproduced, stored or transmitted in any form or by any means, electronic, mechanical, digital or otherwise, except under the terms of the Copyright, Designs and Patents Act 1988 or under terms of a licence issued by the publisher. This book is sold subject to the condition that it shall not, by way of trade or otherwise, be lent, resold or hired out, or otherwise circulated without the publishers prior consent in any form or binding or cover other than that in which it is published and without a similar condition, including this condition, being imposed on the subsequent purchaser.
All requests to the Publisher for permission should be addressed to info@d-azur.com.

First published in Great Britain in 2023 by D'Azur Publishing
Contact: info@d-azur.com Visit www.d-azur.com
ISBN 9798864548738

ACKNOWLEDGEMENTS
The publisher wishes to acknowledge the following people and sources:

Series Editor Elizabeth Absalom. Proofing by Steve Welch, British Newspaper Archive; The Times Archive; Cover Malcolm Watson; p6 Geoff Charles - CND rally, Aberystwyth; DWSav; p10 Quatro Valvole; p12 Franz Heinrich - Flickr: Corkscrew (Alton Towers); p13 Hans van Dijk for Anefo; Streisand (Sony BMG); p13 NASA; p14 Prioryman - Own work; p18 ebay; p19 VARA - 64228-KB-7.png Beeld en Geluidwiki - Gallery: The Beatles; p20 David Jellis; Stuart Halliday;Niels Heidenreich; p21 Malcolm Watson; p25 Sailko and one more author - Own work; p27 Val Vannet; p29 McKlein & BMW; p31 Pexels - https://pixabay.com; p33 Wolfgang Fricke - Own work; p35 Omroepvereniging VARA; p41 Anthony Noble; p45 p47 Jurassica02; p55 HazelAB - Own work; p57 Anthony Conti; Doug Coldwell; p57 Ben Tullis; p61 F. Perroux Zoo de la Palmyre; Jessie Cohen, Smithsonian; p63 Malcolm Watson; p65 Malcolm Asquith; p65 Terry Whalebone; p67 Worshipful Company of Drapers; p73 Andrew Dunn: garethwiscombe; p75 The Royal Mint; p75 Coin Craft:p79 Fotograaf Onbekend / Anefo; p81 Harris Tweed Authority; p83 Malcolm Watson; p85 Tim Green aka atoach; Ian Forshaw/MOD;p87 Vanhoff; Paymaneah R; p89 Royal Air Force; Petri Levälahti/Microsoft; p91 Barts Heritage; p91 open Sandwich; p91 Calendar Customs; p93 Malcolm Watson; p95 VinciosC; p97 AsianGames Swimming; p99 Wes Warren on Unsplash; abi Scott on Unsplash; USGC: p101 Archiv der Stadt Linz; Altaussee Saltmin; p103 iton Rocker - Own work; Reg Mckenna; p107 Ecirphr - Own work; p111 Michael Albov - Michelle L' Amour; p115 Geoff Charles - Aberaman Miners' Training Centre; p121 Diliff - Own work; p127 The Silver Lady Fund;

Whilst we have made every effort to contact copyright holders, should we have made any omission, please contact us so that we can make the appropriate acknowledgement.

CONTENTS

1964 Highlights Of The Year   4-5

1964 The Year You Were Born   6-7

1969 The Year You Were Five   8-9

1975 The Year You Were Eleven   10-11

1980 The Year You Were Sixteen   12-13

1985 The Year You Were Twenty One   14-15

1964 The Major Sporting Events   16-17

1964 The Major Cultural Events   18-19

1964 Science and Nature   20-21

1964 The Lifestyles of Everyday People   22-23

THE YEAR DAY-BY-DAY   **24-127**

The 1964 calendar   128

LIFE IN 1964

Monarch: Queen Elizabeth II
Prime Ministers: Alec Douglas Home (Conservative) (until 16 October). Harold Wilson (Labour)

1964 began under the 13th year of Conservative rule. Alec Douglas-Home presided over a country engulfed in Beatlemania; mini skirts were on the rise; Mods and Rockers took to fighting at the seaside and it was the year The Great Train Robbers were jailed. In October, thirteen years of Tory rule ended when Harold Wilson was elected Labour Prime Minister in the hope of improving poor industrial relations, with a growing number of days lost to strike action and the militant trade unions.

In America, anti-Vietnam war protests were increasing and The Civil Rights Act was made law by President Johnson. The Forth Road Bridge opened; Winston Churchill retired and Radio Caroline, the 'pirate radio station' began broadcasting from a ship just outside UK territorial waters off Suffolk. Elizabeth Taylor married Richard Burton for the first time; BBC aired the first 'Top of the Pops' and BBC 2 took to the air.

Mods (top) and the Forth road bridge (bottom)

FAMOUS PEOPLE WHO WERE BORN IN 1964

12th Jan: Jeff Bezos, Internet entrepreneur
7th Feb: Ray Mears, Woodsman & TV presenter
16th Feb: Christopher Eccleston, British actor
3rd Apr: Nigel Farage, British politician
7th Apr: Russel Crowe, New Zealand born actor
19th Jun: Boris Johnson, British PM
21st Jul: Ross Kemp, British actor
10th Oct: Sarah Lancashire, British actress
21st Nov: Sean Foley, Director, writer, comedian

FAMOUS PEOPLE WHO DIED IN 1964

29th Jan: Alan Ladd, American actor
20th Mar: Brendan Behan, Irish poet & writer
2nd May: Nancy Astor, American born politician
31st Jul: Jim Reeves, American country singer
12th Aug: Ian Fleming, British author
28th Sep: Harpo Marx, American comedian
15th Oct: Cole Porter, American composer
5th Nov: Mabel Lucie Attwell, British illustrator
9th Dec: Edith Sitwell, British poet

News Of The Year

JANUARY The Leyland Motor company sells 450 buses to the Cuban government in a challenge to the United States' embargo of exporting goods to Cuba.

FEBRUARY The C series £10 note is issued for the first time since 1943. This brown note was the first to feature an image of the monarch on the front and the reverse featured the image of a lion.

MARCH After one of the longest criminal trials and the longest jury retrial in English legal history, verdicts are passed on ten men involved in the Great Train Robbery.

APRIL The opening night of 'BBC Two' is disrupted by power cuts. All viewers saw was an announcer apologising from Alexandra Palace.

MAY At a demonstration in Union Square, New York, twelve young men publicly burned their draft cards in the first such act of protest America's involvement in the war in Vietnam.

JUNE In South Africa, Nelson Mandela, along with seven others, is sentenced to life imprisonment and sent to Robben Island prison.

JULY Sir Winston Churchill retires from public life at the age of 89. He was an MP for 63 years and Prime Minister 1940-1945 and 1951-1955.

AUGUST The last judicial hangings take place in the British Isles. Two men are hanged for a murder.

SEPTEMBER Malta, the 'George Cross Island' obtained independence from the UK. It was a *de facto* colony since 1813 and an important naval base for the British.

OCTOBER After thirteen years in power, the Conservatives are beaten by Labour at the General Election and Harold Wilson becomes Prime Minister.

NOVEMBER In the US presidential election, the incumbent, President Lyndon B Johnson defeats the Republican challenger, Barry Goldwater with over 60% of the popular vote.

DECEMBER After breaking the world land speed record in Lake Eyre, South Australia and with only hours to spare on 31st, Donald Campbell broke the world water speed record on Lake Dumbleyung in 'Bluebird'. He is the only person to gain two world records in the same year.

Films and Arts

Sidney Poitier became the first ever Black actor to win an Academy Award for a leading role when he won the Oscar for **Lilies of the Field.**

Julie Andrews stars as **Mary Poppins.** The film is a huge hit and goes on to become Disney's highest-grossing film and to win five Academy Awards.

At the height of Beatlemania, the 'fab four' release and star in their first film, **A Hard Day's Night** which showed 36 hours in the lives of the Beatles as they prepared for a TV performance and Audrey Hepburn and Rex Harrison help **My Fair Lady** reap eight Oscars.

Top of the Pops debuts on BBC television and Dusty Springfield's **I Only Want to Be with You** is the first ever song featured.

Thomson & Co publish the girl's magazine **Jackie** which becomes the best-selling teen-magazine for ten years.

The illustrator **Mabel Lucie Atwell** died. Her trademark style was sentimental, rotund, cuddly infants, used in a wide range of cards, calendars, crockery and nursery equipment, but she also produced a number of posters for London Transport, featuring the children to promote travel to Christmas pantomimes.

1964 THE YEAR

Born in 1964, you were one of 53.9 million people living in Britain and your life expectancy *then* was 71.2 years. You were one of the 18 births per 1,000 population and you had a 2.1% chance of dying as an infant, a rapidly declining chance as this figure in 1950 was almost 31%.

You were at the beginning of an exciting era of individualism, young people had found their voice and were heard. It was the early days of the feminist movement and saw the growth in campaigns against nuclear weapons and the war in Vietnam and, human rights - whilst we were making great strides towards space travel.

In 1946, an Italian baker, Pietro Ferrero, in Alba, an Italian town known for growing hazelnuts, produced a batch of *Pasta Gianduja*.

This paste, a blend of chocolate with 30% hazelnut paste came originally from Turin during Napoleon's regency, eaten as a block or filling for chocolates. Ferrero made a creamy version and in 1964, his son Michele, revamped *Supercrema gianduja* and renamed it Nutella – an instant success.

In 1964, the standard rate of income tax was 7s 9d in the pound (39%). 'Brut' was launched by the American firm Fabergé Inc. and Pop Tarts were first introduced by Kellogg's.

How Much Did It Cost?

The Average Pay:	£915
The Average House:	£3,092
Loaf of White Bread:	1s 2½d (6p)
Pint of Milk:	9d (4p)
Pint of Beer:	2s 3d (11p)
12mnths Road Tax	£15
Gallon of Petrol:	5s 1d (6p/litre)
Newspapers:	5d - 1s (2-5p)
To post a letter in UK:	3d (1p)
TV Licence	£5 Black & White

Most teenagers owned a transistor radio and listened to pirate Radio Caroline, broadcast from the ship anchored off Felixstowe. On TV we were introduced to the Likely Lads and Playschool was launched for the little ones.

YOU WERE BORN

POPULAR MUSIC

For the second successive year, The Beatles had the biggest-selling single of the year with **Can't Buy Me Love**. It spent three weeks at No1.

The group had a total of five top 10 entries, including two No1's from 1963, **She Loves You** and **I Want to Hold Your Hand** plus their fifth and sixth No1's **A Hard Day's Night** and **I Feel Fine**.

JANUARY **Glad All Over** by the Dave Clark Five was their first No1 hit and knocked the Beatles **I Want to Hold Your Hand** off the top spot.

FEBRUARY Bacharach and David wrote **Anyone Who Had a Heart** for Dionne Warwick but her version lost out to Cilla Black's in the UK, which stayed at No1 for three weeks

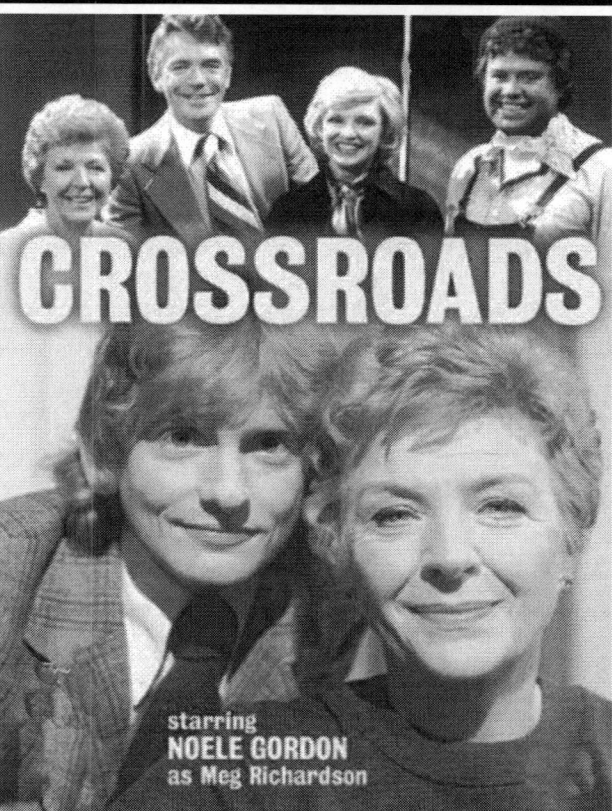

The daily soap opera **Crossroads** began in 1964. Set in a fictional motel in the Midlands the programme became the byword for cheap production values and had huge negative criticism – but despite this, it was loved by millions of regular fans.

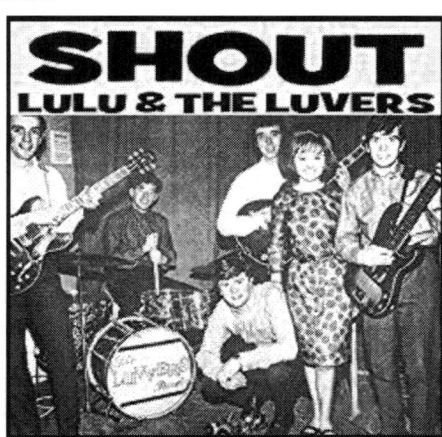

JUNE Scottish singer Lulu has her debut No1 hit with the Isley Brothers' 1959 hit, **Shout**.

JULY **A Hard Day's Night** by the Beatles featured on the soundtrack of their first feature film. The song topped the charts in both the UK and US.

OCTOBER Bare foot Sandie Shaw had her first No1 with **Always Something There to Remind Me**. Written by Bacharach and David, it had previously been 'demoed' by Dionne Warwick.

NOVEMBER **Little Red Rooster** by The Rolling Stones became the first blues standard to reach No1 but within a week Gene Pitney took the top spot with **I'm Gonna be Strong**.

1969 THE YEAR

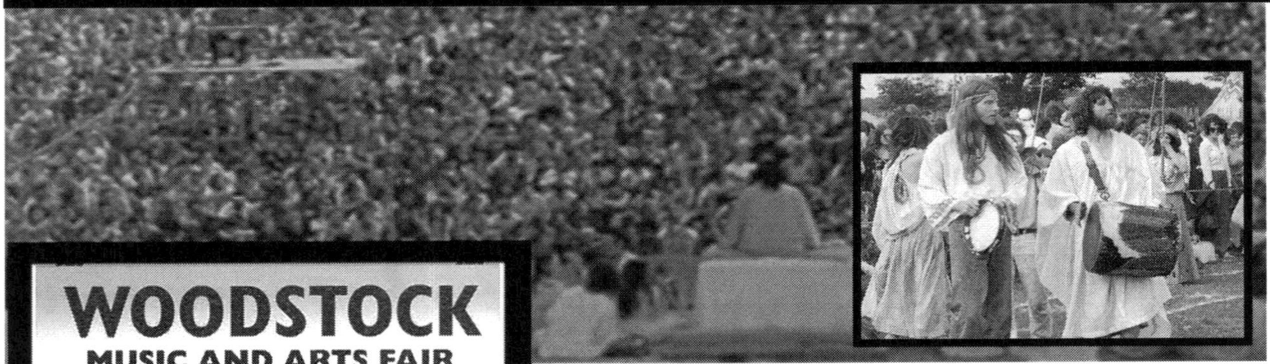

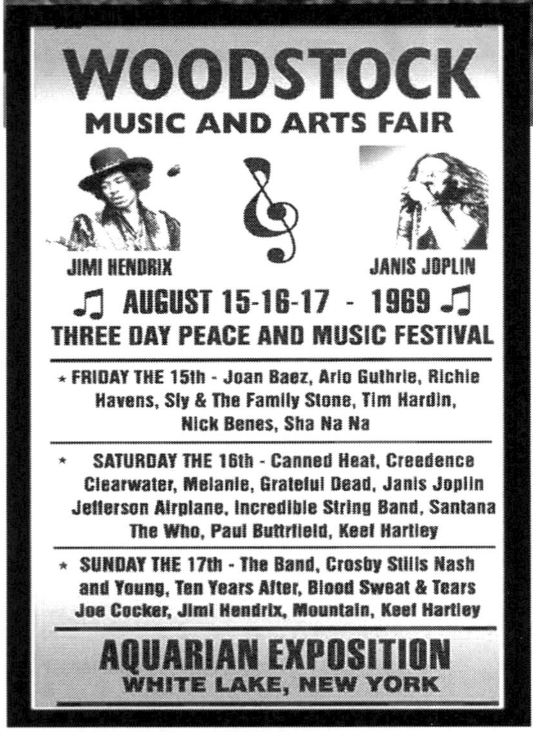

WOODSTOCK
MUSIC AND ARTS FAIR

JIMI HENDRIX

JANIS JOPLIN

♪ AUGUST 15-16-17 - 1969 ♪
THREE DAY PEACE AND MUSIC FESTIVAL

* **FRIDAY THE 15th** - Joan Baez, Arlo Guthrie, Richie Havens, Sly & The Family Stone, Tim Hardin, Nick Benes, Sha Na Na

* **SATURDAY THE 16th** - Canned Heat, Creedence Clearwater, Melanie, Grateful Dead, Janis Joplin Jefferson Airplane, Incredible String Band, Santana The Who, Paul Butterfield, Keef Hartley

* **SUNDAY THE 17th** - The Band, Crosby Stills Nash and Young, Ten Years After, Blood Sweat & Tears Joe Cocker, Jimi Hendrix, Mountain, Keef Hartley

AQUARIAN EXPOSITION
WHITE LAKE, NEW YORK

In 1969 Concorde flew for the first time; the fifty pence piece arrived and there was an all-encompassing excitement of Apollo 11 and Neil Armstrong becoming the 'First Man on the Moon'.

Those left on the ground wanted to 'Make Love not War' and thirty-two acts performed to a crowd of more than 400,000, in sporadic rain, on a dairy farm in New York at the Woodstock music festival.

The nation's girls cried as the Beatles performed together for the last time on a London rooftop.

Young people were influenced by the political climate, they demonstrated in the streets against the Vietnam War, for civil rights and to 'Ban the Bomb'. Outdoor music festivals sprang up all over the country and thousands of, usually mud-caked, teenagers gathered to listen to their favourite artists.

Five In 1969

In 1969 there were no state pre-schools or nurseries, so for most children at five years old, the first day at school was the first time they would have spent the day away from family or friends and for most, because their mother would have been home with them all day, the first time they would be separated.

It could be a very tearful day for both mother and child! But for the child, school life had a routine – calling the register, lessons, playtime and mid-morning, the mostly dreaded 'school milk'. Warmed by the sun or worse, when frozen, warmed by the radiator! Reading, writing and arithmetic were most important; times tables were learnt by rote as was poetry; neat handwriting was practiced daily, and nature study was 'science'.

How Much Did It Cost?

The Average Pay:	£936 (£18 p.w)
The Average House:	£4201
Loaf of White Bread:	1s 8d (8p)
Pint of Milk:	2s 9d (13p)
Pint of Beer:	2s 9d (14p)
12mnths Road Tax	£25
Gallon of Petrol:	6s 6d (33p)
Newspapers:	5d - 1s (2-5p)
To post a letter in UK:	5d (2p)
TV Licence	£6 Black & White £11 Colour

YOU WERE FIVE

POPULAR MUSIC

John Lennon had four UK top 10 singles in 1969, the most of any artist this year. Three of these were as part of The Beatles, **Get Back** and **The Ballad of John and Yoko** topped the charts.

The controversial **Je t'aime... moi non plus** was written in 1967 for Brigitte Bardot but Serge Gainsbourg and Jane Birkin reached number 1 in the UK in October. It was banned in several countries due to its overtly sexual content.

MARCH **Where Do You Go To (My Lovely)?** by Peter Sarstedt is a song about a fictional girl named Marie-Claire who grows up in the backstreets of Naples, becomes a member of the jet-set and goes on to live in Paris. It stayed at No1 for four weeks.

APRIL **I Heard It Through the Grapevine** by Marvin Gaye went to No1 for three weeks and became the biggest hit single on the Motown label.

JULY **Honky Tonk Women** sung by The Rolling Stones topped the charts both in the UK and the US.

AUGUST Creedence Clearwater Revival had two UK top 10 hits this year, including **Bad Moon Rising** which spent three weeks at No1.

OCTOBER The Archies, a fictional American rock band that featured in media produced by, and related to, Archie Comics, took the bubblegum pop genre, **Sugar Sugar,** to No1 for eight weeks.

On July 20, 1969, Neil Armstrong became the first human to step on the moon. He and his co-astronaut Buzz Aldrin stayed for three hours collecting samples of rocks and left the 'Stars and Stripes' flying there.

NOVEMBER **Yester-Me, Yester-You, Yesterday** reaches No2 in the charts and is Stevie Wonder's biggest UK hit at that time

1975 The Year

1975 was a year of many contrasts and new beginnings. Unemployment rose steadily to 1.25 million by August, but the Sex Discrimination and Equal Pay Acts paved the way for a fairer society. Bill Gates founded Microsoft at the tender age of 19, and Margaret Thatcher became the first woman leader of the Conservative Party. The weather was equally astonishing with snow showers as far as London in June. The Sex Pistols made their debut in November establishing Punk Rock on the music scene, while on the TV we watched Fawlty Towers.

Package tours to sunny, warm and cheap holiday destinations were very popular. Companies such as Thompson, Horizon, Global and Clarksons all used chartered planes to fly families to booming resorts Once there, holiday makers found that in addition to the sun and sand, food and drink was much cheaper than in the UK and this led to the rapid decline in UK seaside resorts and boom in once sleepy fishing villages such as Benidorm.

On 3rd November the Forties Field was inaugurated by Her Majesty Queen Elizabeth at Aberdeen. It is the largest oilfield to be discovered so far in the British sector of the North Sea. Initially the production rate was 10,000 barrels per day, with a prospective increase to 400,000 barrels per day in the future, fuelling hopes of a steady return to better times for the country's economy.

Eleven In 1975

Eleven-year-olds in 1975 went from being the 'king pins' at primary school to the 'newcomers' at their secondary school. The 11+ selective exam was almost totally phased out and comprehensive schools were the norm for most children. It was the start of growing up but at home there was still plenty of fun. Chopper bikes were a status symbol; space hoppers were still 'cool' enough and there were video games and colour TV.

How Much Did It Cost?

The Average Pay:	£3.380 (£65 p.w)
The Average House:	£9,500
Loaf of White Bread:	15p
Pint of Milk:	7p
Pint of Beer:	18p
Gallon of Petrol:	73p (15p/litre)
12mnths Road Tax	£40
Newspapers:	5p
To post a letter in UK:	7p
TV Licence	£8 Black & White £18 Colour

You Were Eleven

Popular Music

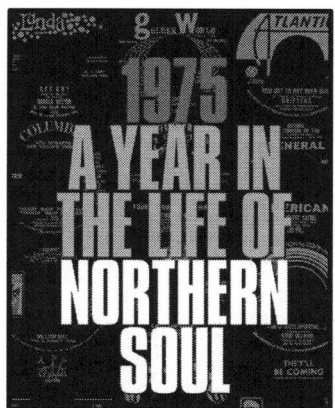 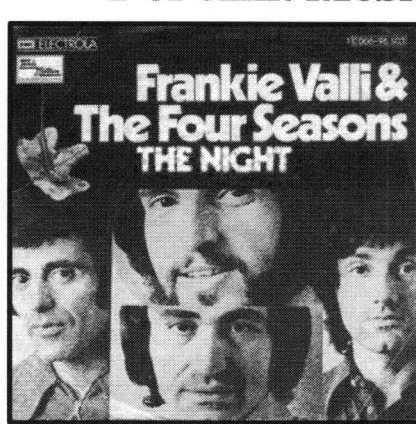 

1975 saw the burgeoning of Northern Soul in the industrial towns of England. Focusing on the rare 'B' side records of America, in particular early Motown label songs it had cult status in venues such as Wigan Casino, Blackpool Mecca, The Twisted Wheel in Manchester and The Torch in Stoke. One of the iconic records of the movement was **The Night** by Frankie Valli & The Four Seasons released in May.

FEBRUARY Make Me Smile by Steve Harley & Cockney Rebel was the first release by the re-invented band which was disbanded in 1974

MARCH The Bay City Rollers had 3 chart singles in this year, with **Bye Bye Baby** being the bestselling record of the year. The Scottish group from Edinburgh boosted not only record sales but also sales of anything tartan to the plaid hungry teenage fans!

JUNE I'm Not in Love by 10cc was a top ten hit for 7 weeks, but remained a firm romantic favourite for years afterwards

AUGUST The second bestselling single of this year was Rod Stewart's **Sailing**, which stayed in the chart for 4 weeks, and was also used as the theme for the television programme about the Royal Navy warship 'Ark Royal'.

SEPTEMBER Hold Me Close written and performed by singer and actor David Essex stayed at No1 for 3 weeks.

NOVEMBER American country music singer Glen Campbell released **Rhinestone Cowboy** which was hugely popular with both country and pop audiences.

DECEMBER In the depths of winter Demis Roussos hit he charts with **Happy to Be on an Island in the Sun.**

1980 THE YEAR

In 1980, Margaret Thatcher battled with the Trade Unions; 90,000 steelworkers went on strike for the first time since 1926 and state benefit to strikers was halved; Zimbabwe gained independence; the sixpence coin was withdrawn from circulation; the first CND rally was held at Greenham Common; Radio Caroline ran aground and sank and Mrs Thatcher declared, "The lady's not for turning."

But there was plenty to smile about; Alton Towers theme park opened; Robin Cousins won gold in figure skating; ITV had a record audience of 23.5 million for "Live and Let Die"; "Children in Need" began and "Postman Pat" introduced his cat to us.

Alton Towers. The Corkscrew

UFOs in the Forest

On 26 December 1980, several US Air force personnel stationed near the east gate at RAF Woodbridge, reported they had seen "lights" apparently descending into nearby Rendlesham Forest. They initially thought it was a downed aircraft but, upon investigation, they saw what they described as a glowing object, metallic in appearance, with coloured lights.

After daybreak on the morning of December 27, servicemen returned to a small clearing in the forest and found three small impressions on the ground in a triangular pattern, as well as burn marks and broken branches on nearby trees.

The 'Rendlesham Forest Incident' made headline news and theories suggest it was either an actual alien visitation, a secret military aircraft, a misinterpretation of natural lights, the beam of Orfordness Lighthouse, or just a hoax.

LIFE AT SIXTEEN

Sixteen in 1980, you could leave school; join the army; legally buy cigarettes as well as smoke them; pubs were only open lunchtimes and evenings, and you couldn't have a beer unless an "adult" over 18 bought it for you and you were eating a meal.

Long, straight hair was still 'de rigeur' for boys and girls and fashion was soft 'New Romantic' whilst carrying on the trend for sportswear, girls increasingly wore stylish gym wear in their day-to-day life.

HOW MUCH DID IT COST?

The Average Pay	£6,188 (£119 p.w.)
The Average House	£22.700
Loaf of White Bread	36p
Pint of Milk	17p
Pint of Beer	41p
Gallon of Petrol	£1.28 (27p/litre)
Newspapers	12p-15p
To Post a Letter in UK	12p
12 Mths Road Tax	£60
TV Licence	B/W £12 Colour £34

You Were Sixteen

Popular Music

The 1979 Christmas No 1, **Another Brick in the Wall** by Pink Floyd, written as a protest against rigid schooling, remained at number-one for the first two weeks of 1980. The first new No 1 of the year was **Brass in Pocket** by The Pretenders. Sting and his band, The Police, had the bestselling single of the year with **Don't Stand So Close to Me** which spent four weeks at No 1. ABBA reached the top ten with three singles, including the two No 1s, **The Winner Takes It All** and **Super Trouper**.

FEBRUARY Kenny Rogers stayed at No 1 for two weeks with **Coward of the County.** The song became a massive 'cross over' hit, appealing to diverse audiences.

APRIL Dexy's Midnight Runners' second single, **Geno,** was their first No 1 and they had another top ten entry with **There, There My Dear** in August.

MAY The Eurovision Song Contest was won by Johnny Logan with **What's Another Year** and the single reached No 1 for two weeks

Johnny Logan

SEPTEMBER **D.I.S.C.O.** by Ottawan got us dancing, reached No 2 in the charts and ended the year as one of the five top selling singles of 1980.

OCTOBER Barbra Streisand had her only UK No 1 single with **Woman in Love**, which became the year's second bestselling single.

DECEMBER Following his death on the 8th, John Lennon's **(Just Like) Starting Over** hit the No 1 spot.

13

1985 The Year

1985 was a year with many tragedies. 55 people are killed in the Manchester Air Disaster; 56 people died in the Bradford City F.C. fire and 39 died in the Heysel Stadium Disaster. There was football hooliganism; Brixton riots and scientists found the ozone hole in the atmosphere but the devastating Miners' Strike ends after one year; Live Aid pop concerts raise over £50m for famine relief in Ethiopia; the first mobile phone calls in the UK are made; the first UK heart and lung transplant is carried out and the Sinclair C5 'bicycle' has a seven month life!

The Sinclair C5

Fashion had moved away from the 70s styles and pop stars like Cyndi Lauper were bringing in an entirely new look, especially for the young. Brightly coloured accessories like sunglasses, bangles and hoop earrings were a necessity. Teased hair, loud makeup and neon were all important.

When You Were 21

Twenty-one in 1985, you were enjoying the 1980's fitness craze. Celebrities made aerobics videos; Health Clubs and Gyms, predominantly for men, became the place to be and to be seen whilst women exercised in the privacy of their own home, to a well-worn VHS copy of 'Jane Fonda's Workout', or to Diana Moran 'The Green Goddess', who appeared on TV screens wearing her trade-mark green leotard telling millions of BBC Breakfast viewers to 'wake up and shape up' with her aerobics routines.

How Much Did It Cost?

The Average Pay:	£11,544 (£222 pw)
The Average House:	£43,000
Loaf of White Bread:	40p
Pint of Milk:	23p
Pint of Beer:	77p
Gallon of Petrol:	£1.99 (45p/litre)
12mnths Road Tax:	£100
Newspapers:	18-23p
To post a letter in UK:	17p
TV Licence	£18 Black & White £58 Colour

You Were 21

Popular Music

The Dire Straits album **Brothers in Arms** was released and becomes the first compact disc to sell over 1,000,000 copies. Jennifer Rush had the bestselling single of the year with **The Power of Love** and Madonna had a total of eight top ten hits. **Into the Groove** was her first UK No 1. Foreigner was the first No 1 of the year with **I Want to Know What Love Is.**

JANUARY **I Know Him So Well** by Elaine Paige and Barbara Dickson was No 1 for four weeks into February and became the second bestselling single of the year.

APRIL **We Are the World**, the charity single by USA for Africa, stayed at No 1 for two weeks. Written by Michael Jackson and Lionel Richie, it sold in excess of 20m copies.

JUNE A special recording of **You'll Never Walk Alone** was made after the Bradford City F.C. fire. Performed by The Crowd featuring Gerry Marsden, Paul McCartney and others.

SEPTEMBER Midge Ure, co-writer of the charity single **Do They Know it's Christmas** has his only No 1 as a solo artist with **If I Was.**

FEBRUARY Bruce Springsteen added 'uptempo' synthesizer riffs to his sound for the first time in **Dancing in the Dark.** From his album **Born in the USA,** it reached No 4 in the UK but became his biggest hit worldwide.

DECEMBER The Pet Shop Boys released their **West End Girls,** inspired by TS Eliot's poem, The Waste Land, but it did not peak at No 1 until the new year.

1964

SPORTING HEADLINES

FEBRUARY Cassius Clay won his first world **Heavyweight Boxing** title when Sonny Liston failed to come out for Round 7 at the Convention Center, Miami Beach.

Australian Richie Benaud ended his 63 **Test Cricket** career in the 5th Test, Australia v South Africa, in Sydney. The match was drawn.

MARCH The **Cheltenham Gold Cup** was won by the Irish thoroughbred, Arkle. It was the first of his three consecutive wins.

APRIL In the **US Masters Tournament**, Augusta, Arnold Palmer won by 6 shots from Dave Marr and Jack Nicklaus to become the first 4-time winner of the Masters, his 7th and final major victory.

MAY The **FA Cup Final** was won by West Ham United who beat Preston North End by 3 goals to two.

JULY In an all-Australian final, Roy Emerson beat Fred Stolle in the **Men's Wimbledon Singles**. This was the first of Emerson's two straight Wimbledon titles.
Maria Bueno of Brazil won her third **Wimbledon Ladies Singles** title beating Margaret Smith of Australia.

The **Tour de France** was won by Jacques Anquetil of France, the first cyclist to win the Tour five times. 1957 and 1961-64

SEPTEMBER The New York Yacht Club retained the **America's Cup** as 'Constellation' defeated the British challenger, 'Sovereign' by four races to one.

OCTOBER The **Formula One** drivers' championship was decided at the Mexican Grand Prix when Graham Hill was delayed after a collision, Jim Clark was forced to stop with an oil leak on the last lap, and Ferrari signalled Bandini to let John Surtees through into the second place which gave him the championship by one point from Hill.

John Surtees, winner of the 1964 F1 Championship

SPORTING EVENTS

THE GREATEST

On 25th February 1964, a crowd of 8,300 excited spectators gathered in the Convention Hall arena at Miami Beach, to see if Cassius Clay, who was nicknamed the 'Louisville Lip,' could put his money where his mouth was. He had predicted he was going to '*float like a butterfly, sting like a bee*' and knock out the reigning World Heavyweight Boxing champion, Sonny Liston, in the eighth round. The fearsome Liston, who had twice beaten the former champion Floyd Patterson in one round only, was an 8-to-1 favourite to demolish this brash youngster equally quickly. However, the 22-year-old 'braggart', dancing and dodging away from Liston's powerful swings whilst managing to deliver punishingly quick jabs to his opponent's head, shocked the pundits and stole the crown with a technical knockout in a sensational end to the fight when Sonny Liston retired before the start of the seventh round.

Cassius Marcellus Clay Jr. was born in Louisville, Kentucky in 1942 and started boxing when he was 12. Having won over 100 bouts in amateur competitions, he then won the 'International Golden Gloves' heavyweight title in 1959 and was entered into the Olympic Games in Rome in 1960, where he won a heavyweight Gold Medal. Clay turned professional and won his first 19 bouts which then gave him the right to challenge Sonny Liston for the World Heavyweight title.

Not long after he won this world title, Cassius Clay was at a gathering with his friend Malcolm X, the leader of the African American Muslim group known as the 'Nation of Islam' and a few days later, he announced he was joining the organisation. A descendant of formerly enslaved ancestors, he rejected his family name – given by the slave owners – and took the Muslim name of Muhammad Ali.

1964

ZULU WARS

This year saw Michael Caine in his first major role in the film **Zulu**, an epic war film set at the Battle of Rorke's Drift between the British Army and the Zulus in 1879.

The film was not shot at Rorke's Drift however, but 90 miles away in the Royal Natal National Park, a far more mountainous and scenic site than the real one. Many of the Zulus, who were hired as extras for the film, had never seen a motion picture prior to filming and contrary to popular belief, they were not paid in cattle, but were paid in full in Rand.

The Zulu chief who later became an influential South African political leader, Mangosuthu Buthelezi, played in the film, the Zulu King Cetshwayo kaMpande, who was his great-grandfather.

THE ENGLISH NANNY

Mary Poppins floated onto cinema screens in the musical fantasy film based on P. L. Traver's book series. Julie Andrews made her feature film debut as the Nanny who does her best to improve the lives of the dysfunctional London family with her unique ways.

The film was shot entirely at the Disney Studios in California using painted London background scenes whilst Dick Van Dyke played the jovial chimney sweep with a less than totally convincing cockney accent!

The word, 'supercalifragilisticexpialidocious' used in the film when 'you have nothing to say', was added to the OED with the meaning, 'extraordinarily good; wonderful.' Which could sum up the film, which became the highest-grossing film of the year and, at the time of its release, Disney's highest-grossing film ever.

Cultural Events

The Shot Marilyns

Having a fascination with Hollywood and fame, Andy Warhol began immortalising Marilyn Monroe in his work after her death and had painted five silk screen portraits of her, each with a different coloured background, which he was storing in his studio loft, 'The Factory'.

Four of these five paintings would become perhaps the most famous works he ever created, after an incident that left bullet holes through Ms. Monroe's forehead.

The Factory was always buzzing with artists, photographers and writers by day and by night, Warhol would often throw rowdy parties for celebrities in the New York Scene. One night, a performance artist saw the stack of four of the paintings and asked if she could shoot them. Instead of producing a camera, she produced a revolver and formed The Shot Marilyns.

The Beatles Go Global

After a successful UK tour in the early part of the year, the Beatles embarked on their very first world tour, first stop, Copenhagen in Denmark. But this first concert was not performed by the Fab Four! Ringo Starr had been taken ill the previous day with severe tonsillitis and hospitalised for a few days in London.

Whilst John, George and Paul had wanted to postpone, their manager Brian Epstein and producer George Martin, had insisted that 'the show must go on' and found drummer, Jimmie Nicol, to stand in for Ringo until he had recovered enough to join them ten days later in Melbourne, Australia. The second stage of the World tour, the United States and Canada and was a fantastic success. Beatlemania had crossed the Atlantic.

1964

A New Language

John George Kemeny and Thomas Eugene Kurtz introduced the first programme in BASIC (Beginners' All-purpose Symbolic Instruction Code), a user-friendly high-level programming language. Programming languages are systems for instructing computers which can be text-based or graphical, with specifications defining their syntax and meaning.

BASIC was aimed at making computing accessible to non-scientific students and the initial version featured just 14 simple commands with straightforward names and easy to understand syntax resembling spoken English.

Because of their complexity, before BASIC, computers were primarily the domain of mathematicians and scientists and this breakthrough language paved the way for the first personal computers, providing an accessible means to communicate with machines. BASIC's early applications were simulations and mathematical problem-solving.

Atari BASIC Listing for a little spaceship game.
Line numbers are on the left followed by an instruction.
When it starts, this happens:
• Line 1000 sets foreground and background colors and hiding the cursor. In lines
• Lines 1010–1020, the »sprite« for the little spaceship is created.
• Lines 1025–1040 make a title screen and wait for the joystick button to be pressed.
• Line 1045 clears the screen and returns to the main program starting in line 20 .. And it continues until 'game over' in Line 535.

The Forth Road Bridge

In September, the Queen and the Duke of Edinburgh opened the Forth Road Bridge, at the time, the longest steel suspension bridge in the world outside of the United States. It replaced the ancient ferry service which carried vehicles, cyclists and pedestrians across the Firth of Forth from Edinburgh to Fife. The bridge used 210,000 tons of concrete; is 2,512 metres long with the longest span of 1,0006 metres; 33 metres wide; 156 metres high and cost £15.1 million to build. It has 9 miles (14 km) of dual-carriageway approach roads incorporating 24 individual bridges.

The first river crossing at the site of the bridge was made in the 11th century by Queen Margaret, consort of King Malcolm III, who founded a ferry service to transport pilgrims from Edinburgh to Dunfermline Abbey and St Andrews.

SCIENCE AND NATURE

THE LEANING TOWER OF PISA

In February, the Italian government asked for suggestions to save their famous tourist attraction, the Leaning Tower of Pisa, from collapse. The top of the 180-foot tower was now hanging 17 feet south of the base, and the tilt was increasing fractionally each year leaving the Tower in danger of falling.

The Tower was built to house the bells of the vast cathedral of the Piazza dei Miracoli and construction began in 1173. At this time Pisa was a major trading power and one of the richest cities in the world and this bell tower was to be the most magnificent in Europe.

However, construction stopped and started over the following 197 years and it was not officially completed, already leaning more than three feet, until about 1370.

THE GREAT ALASKAN EARTHQUAKE

The 'Great Alaskan Earthquake' took place on Good Friday, March 27th. The resulting ground fissures, collapsing structures and devastating tsunamis and landslides, caused over 130 deaths and massive property damage. Geological surveys taken immediately afterwards showed that parts of the Alaskan coast sank up to eight feet, other parts rose up to 38 feet and much of the coast moved 50 feet towards the ocean.

Coastal forests plunged below sea level and were destroyed by salt water. It was the strongest earthquake ever recorded in North America and struck Alaska's Prince William Sound, about 74 miles southeast of Anchorage. With a magnitude of 9.2, the earthquake wobbled Seattle's Space Needle some 1,200 miles away and was so powerful it registered in all but three U.S. states.

1964 LIFESTYLES OF

European style had already begun to dominate the fashion world and whilst, for older people, the look in 1964 was still reminiscent of the 50's - conservative and restrained, the American First Lady, Jackie Kennedy, had a huge influence on a whole generation. She wore elegant outfits, suits and simple yet stylish shift dresses in block colours. She paired these with the pill box hats she popularised, button earrings and white gloves and embraced the bouffant hairstyle which, with the help of Audrey Hepburn and Brigitte Bardot, developed into the iconic 'beehive.'

Young men were influenced by the Beatles, who moved away from leather jackets, polo necks and cowboy boots to the grey 'collarless' suit which became the most iconic of Beatle looks. It was usually worn by the fab four in grey but also made several appearances in black and not to forget, mop top hair, made famous by the Fab Four and imitated around the country.

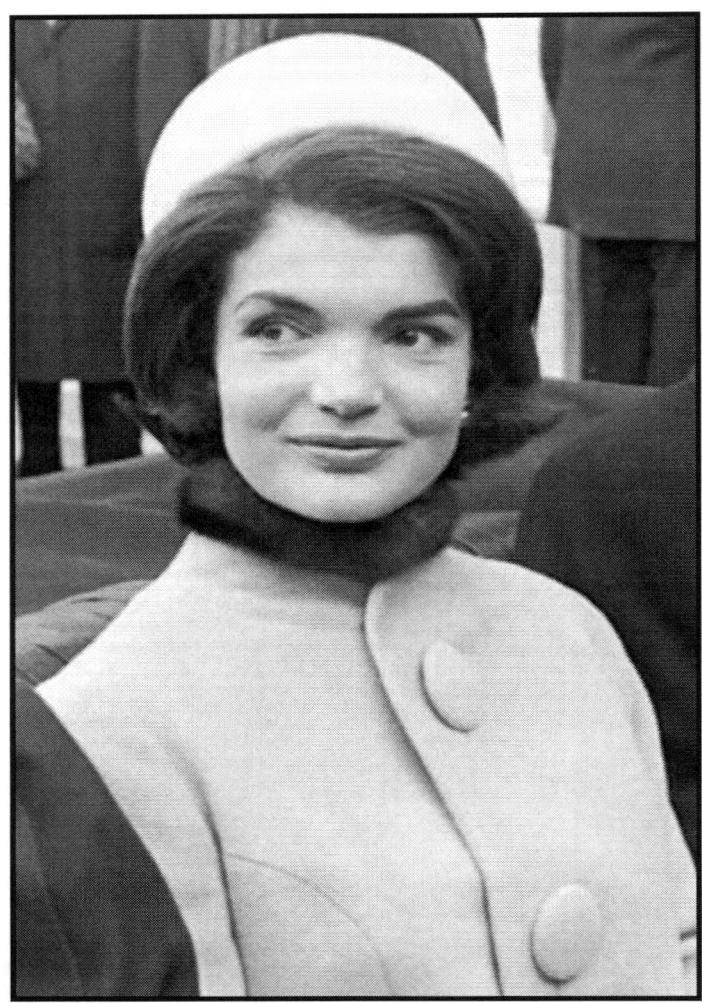

As a child you could spend your pocket money, probably still about 6d a week, on your favourite sweet treats. Rolls of Love Hearts were put in their special Christmas Crackers by Swizzels. They were such a success that the fizzy sweets with their fun messages became permanent, selling at 3d a pack.

One of the best sweets for sharing were Rowntree's Fruit Gums. Their famous slogan: "Don't forget the Fruit Gums, Mum" was changed to "Chum", not "Mum" in 1961 when the company became aware of accusations of 'pester power' and didn't want the nation's mothers disapproving of them as a brand.

Treets, Peanut, Toffee or Chocolate, which 'Melt in your mouth, not in your hand', and more and more sweets in packets rather than being weighed out by the shopkeeper from jars and handed over in little paper bags.

EVERYDAY PEOPLE

Your holiday during the 6 week summer break was likely to be in Britain. Holiday camps such as Butlins with their 'Red Coats' offered hours of fun, coaches could take you to the seaside and owning a caravan was becoming popular too.

In 1964 the nuclear family was still the norm, father out at work and mother busy with the housework which was time consuming before the general possession of electrical labour-saving devices. Washing up was done by hand and laundry gradually moved to machines over the decade. Twin tubs, one for washing and one for spinning, became popular in the late 60's and were usually wheeled into the kitchen to be attached to the cold tap and afterwards, have the waste-water emptied into the sink. The 'housewife' had to be at home to transfer the wet washing from the washing tub to the spinning tub.

Goods came to you. The milkman delivered the milk to your doorstep, the baker brought the baskets of bread to the door, the greengrocer delivered and the 'pop man' came once a week with 'dandelion and burdock', 'cherryade' or 'cream soda' and the rag and bone man visited the street for your recycling.

January 1st - 7th 1964

IN THE NEWS

Wednesday 1 — **"Moonlit Escape"** The RAF Mountain Rescue brought to safety at last the two-man crew of a survey aircraft owned by a private company that crashed in the Peak District last week. Both men sustained serious but recoverable injuries.

Thursday 2 — **"Cypriot Abrogation"** The President of Cyprus has announced that Cyprus would no longer honour the 1960 treaty between itself, Britain, Greece, and Turkey following acts of aggression and 'imposition' by Turkey.

Friday 3 — **"Peak Power"** The Minister for Power has unveiled plans to rework the proposed overhead power lines in the Peak District National Park, which attracted a lot of protest, into an underground project.

Saturday 4 — **"An Added Bonus"** In elation, workers carried their boss home from a factory after receiving surprise bonuses worth over £250,000, and the owner, millionaire Mr Joe Bamford also paid the income tax due on the bonuses.

Sunday 5 — **"The Pope's Pilgrimage"** For the first time since apostolic times, the Pope will leave Italy on a pilgrimage to the geographical origins of the Christian faith.

Monday 6 — **"Robot Eye Tube Tickets"** Trials have got underway for an automated ticketing system to be implemented in the London Underground, with the scanning of 'robot eyes' to ensure valid tickets. The full roll out of the system is set to be completed by 1970.

Tuesday 7 — **"Cuban British Bus Purchase"** The Leyland Motor Corporation has agreed to the sale of over 400 buses, worth approximately £10 million, to the Cuban government, despite the efforts of the US government to diplomatically isolate the country.

HERE IN BRITAIN

"Oxfam Refusal"

Oxfam have demanded that a collection box given to Miss Mandy Rice Davies be given back, after the author requested donations into the box in return for signed copies of her book, 'The Mandy Report'.

Oxfam's statement against commercial collection has been challenged by Miss Rice Davies, who has said *"I have never heard such rubbish in my life. I shall continue to autograph copies, only I shall put the money in a soup plate or something. Children that Oxfam are helping will still benefit whether some fuddy-duddies in London like it or not."*

AROUND THE WORLD

"Give Away Games"

US supermarkets are employing new marketing techniques to win over customers, after market research showed the ineffectiveness of the commonly used 'trading stamps' rewarding loyalty. Instead, customers will be offered the opportunity to play a number of games with enticing names such as 'Instant Bucks', 'Split the Dollar' and 'The Price is Right'.

Although the stamps will remain, the new games have proved to be remarkably effective, with supermarkets in the US now in competition with one another for customers based on the ingenuity of their games.

GOYA ASHES

What is believed to be the ashes of the recently stolen Goya painting of the Duke of Wellington have been recovered in a cardboard box in the main cloakroom onboard a train at Victoria Station. Although on preliminary examination the ashes showed no traces of canvas, they have been sent to New Scotland Yard for further investigation. Inside the box was a note with *'Last of the Goya'* written across the front. This comes following the thief's 'Robin Hood-esque' notion of demanding the *'ransom for charity'* and payment into five separate charities of his choosing; the criminal has said that *'I am offering three-pennyworth of old Spanish firewood in exchange for £140,000 of human happiness'*, referring to the demanded ransom for the painting. In this vein, it becomes unlikely that the ashes found on the train in Victoria are in fact the remains of Goya's painting, but it is nonetheless important for proper examination.

The painting, stolen since 1961, remains one of the great art theft mysteries of the decade, notable enough to even gain a reference in the James Bond movie, Dr No. The portrait of the Duke of Wellington, hung just three weeks prior to its theft, made an inconspicuous appearance in the underground lair of the latest Bond villain in the movie, a subtle yet comedic hark to the unsolved nature of the crime. At the scene of the crime in the National Museum, police found the bathroom window open, which is likely how the thief got in and out of the building. Since the heist, the perpetrator has appeared in the media once a year reasserting his demands for a ransom in return for the safe return of the painting, to be paid in full to a conglomerate of charities.

January 8th – 14th 1964

IN THE NEWS

Wednesday 8 — **"The Merry-Go-Round"** The British railway network is set for a renovation following a new agreement for the cheaper transportation of coal to power stations.

Thursday 9 — **"Double the Power"** By 1970, the UK's power output will have doubled, with the implementation of 32 new power stations across the country, costing approximately £400 million a year. The plans come following the ever-increasing demand for electricity in Britain, with the figure also expected to double by then.

Friday 10 — **"Two-Pedal Control"** Medium and light class cars have at last moved towards automatic transmission, with Ford's release of the Borg-Warner Model 35 automatic transmission as an optional extra to their range of Cortinas and Corsairs.

Saturday 11 — **"Nuclear Test Fleet"** Britain is the latest of the NATO countries to agree to a multi-national naval program of a manned nuclear fleet.

Sunday 12 — **"Panama Palava"** The ongoing violence on the Panama Canal border in Panama City, has led US delegates to attempt to find peaceful solutions. The US is seeking the withdrawal of all troops and an official agreement between America and the Republic.

Monday 13 — **"Weather Stops Train Travel"** Over forty-eight English counties were hit by snowstorms throughout the day and night causing severe delays and damage to the railway lines. Sussex was the county worst affected.

Tuesday 14 — **"Nuclear Crash"** During an intense snowstorm over Maryland, an American bomber carrying a crew of five and two unarmed nuclear weapons, crashed with no fatalities. Authorities confirmed that there was no risk of explosion as the bombs were unarmed.

HERE IN BRITAIN

"Heavyweight Children"

Doctors across the city of Nottingham have reported an 'obesity epidemic' in young people. Over ninety school children have been categorised as overweight, with some weighing in at more than twenty stone.

School doctors are reportedly unable to ascertain the true weight of some students, with scales only going up to twenty stone, but there was at least one 14-year-old and one 15-year-old girl at a local school who exceeded that weight and were unable to participate in Physical Education classes, or even walk to school.

AROUND THE WORLD

"Snowless Winter"

In a desperate attempt to get the country ready for hosting the Winter Olympics in three weeks' time, Austrian soldiers have been laying down artificial snow on the mountains, following the largely snowless winter experienced.

Austria has undergone their warmest winter on record with no fresh snowfall for over a month and instead, snow is being transported from the high mountains down to the valleys and smaller peaks where the games will be held. Authorities have assured that there is enough snow, but the process of transferring it is no mean feat.

Devil's Dyke Development

Plans for development of a sea lion pool and model village have been dropped by developer Mr Leslie Kramer following what he calls *'misguided opposition'* to the plans. Mr Kramer, a self-proclaimed preservationist, even joined a preservation group protesting his own initial plans, and confirming his change in direction when it came to adapting the ancient site.

The Devil's Dyke is an area of the South Downs near Brighton, often classified as an area of outstanding natural beauty, with 365-degree views of largely undisturbed English countryside. The valley itself acts as the largest and deepest dry valley in the whole of the UK, thus its name derives from the belief that the Devil himself dug the chasm to drown the inhabitants of The Weald. Local folklore describes the valley as being not only the work of the Devil, but also the burial site, with two humps at the bottom of the valley supposedly marking the grave of the Devil and his wife. Legend says that if a person runs backwards around the humps seven times in quick succession, the Devil will appear. The Dyke was exceptionally popular in the 18th and 19th Centuries, with over 30,000 Victorian tourists visiting on one day in 1893.

Kramer's new plans move away from a sea lion pool, a 35 ft model of the Egyptian Abu Simbel Temple and a model village to a more muted garden containing models of fairy-tale characters. The Society of Sussex Downsmen have denounced the scheme as *'artificial and completely discordant with the peace and charm associated with the idea of natural beauty'* which has in turn forced Kramer to stand down his plans. He claimed that he wanted to return to the area its tourist, *'funfair-type'* nature it had gained in the Victorian Era.

January 15th – 21st 1964

IN THE NEWS

Wednesday 15 — **"1,300 Men on Strike"** A five-hour attempt to reach settlement between the South Wales Steel Works company and the Engineering Union has broken down; over 1,300 men have been on strike since before Christmas.

Thursday 16 — **"Spinning Success"** A 6% rise in the cotton industry workforce has been reported for the first time this decade following a steady decline in the industry since the war. Production has seen a 10% increase in line with the rising numbers.

Friday 17 — **"Going Cheap"** Following the government's plans to make resale price maintenance of products including cigarettes, whisky and chocolate illegal, many supermarkets have immediately dropped prices to avoid penalties.

Saturday 18 — **"Cigarette Supply Stoppage"** In the immediate aftermath of supermarkets dropping the retail price of cigarettes, The Imperial Tobacco Company have threatened injunctions to many local shops, calling for the maintenance of their prices.

Sunday 19 — **"Fog Blankets"** The most widespread fog of the winter has swept across Britain, covering everywhere, with the exception of central London and Northumberland. The visiting Sultan of Zanzibar's plane was forced to be diverted twice.

Monday 20 — **"40,000 Tons of Gas"** The Eastern Gas Board has proposed the importing of over 40,000 tons of gas from the USA to help supply towns in Norfolk and north Suffolk.

Tuesday 21 — **"A Penny a Day"** The Association of the British Pharmaceutical Industry has revealed in a leaflet that contrary to claims of critics, the taxpayer pays the equivalent of one penny per day per person to fund the NHS. This compares to 3d on smoking, and 2d on drinking.

HERE IN BRITAIN

"Heart Over Brawn"

Over 50 removal men have gone back to school for a series of lectures by the Institute of the Warehouse and Removal Industry on how to ease the moving process woes of housewives watching their treasured possessions being uprooted.

With England becoming ever more footloose, the institute feels the need to increase the effectiveness of its workers, by training the typically large strong men, in the ways of gentle social interaction and sensitivity when it comes to the movers' property by stressing the importance of building trust in the first ten minutes.

AROUND THE WORLD

"New York Transport Chaos"

Americans across the East Coast have been forced to prepare for the most severe wintry weather of the season, following extreme snowfall of up to an astonishing 27 inches. In New York City, over 13 inches of snow have been recorded in the last 36 hours, with temperatures plummeting to record lows.

Over 100 people have lost their lives and 3,000 passengers have been stranded at Kennedy International Airport due to the unprepared nature of emergency services to deal with such extremities. The conditions are set to only worsen in the coming days.

THE MONTE CARLO RALLY

Having completed the last five stages of the Monte Carlo Rally, made up of over 3,000 corners, for the first time ever, a Mini Cooper S has crossed the finish line to win the 1964 rally. Driven by Irishman Patrick 'Paddy' Hopkirk and his co-driver Henry Liddon the little Mini cruised to victory in the face of adversity, racing against almost 300 far more powerful cars on the gruelling circuit.

The British-built, front wheel drive Mini Cooper S cars, proved to be nimble and effective at dealing with the more driver-focused stages, and the new implementation of over 30 different choices of studded tyre proved to suit the little chassis. The cars were fitted with special heated windscreens, an innovation putting them at a significant advantage over the competition. A thin layer of gold is sandwiched by two layers of glass, and small metal strips run horizontally across the screen, which are in turn connected to an electrical system providing heat and preventing the windscreen from icing up.

Conditions this year are the worst they have been for over a decade, with Graham Hill commenting on how the temperatures were so low *'that the ink in my ballpoint pen froze';* he and his co-driver Ian Walker were amongst the large number of drivers not to make the final checkpoint, merely two thirds of the original starting grid making it through to the final stage. The Russians however, failed the previous rounds not through lack of skill or car trouble, but through their inability to speak the French language, with road signs and signposts being incomprehensible to most of the co-drivers. It appeared that the Russians were ill-equipped, with maps only as far as Holland and a severe lack of detail in French road maps.

JANUARY 22ND - 28TH 1964

Wednesday 22 — "Fogged In" There have been over 200 reported crashes on British roads after severe fog swept across more than 50 counties. The M1 was coated in over 26 miles of icy surface.

Thursday 23 — "Territorial Army Reboot" The Ministry of defence have announced new roles for the territorial army, giving them more responsibility for the support and reinforcement of the British Army of the Rhine, together with a new firefighting role.

Friday 24 — "A Switchboard in Space" The space satellite 'Relay II' was launched in the hope of linking communications between North America, South America, Europe and Asia. At its maximum height, the satellite will be over 4,600 miles above the ground.

Saturday 25 — "The 30 Mile City" Plans were revealed by the government for the building of a 30-mile-long city stretching between County Durham and Northumberland. The city would have a population of 2.5 million.

Sunday 26 — "Gorilla Escape" Two gorillas, who escaped their private zoo at the home of a wealthy landowner in Canterbury, have been recaught after five hours of freedom roaming the estate; they were guided back to their enclosure using water jets and sticks.

Monday 27 — "School Leavers" After the preliminary report was published almost four years ago, the House of Commons has finally passed the law enforcing children to remain in school until 16 years of age, up from 15.

Tuesday 28 — "Mersey Maniacs Banned" British railways have suspended the usual special services for football excursions from Liverpool due to the '*Disgraceful behaviour of the Merseyside maniacs*' involving vandalism and hooliganism onboard the designated trains.

HERE IN BRITAIN
"Gaol for Sale"

The 32-year lease for the island of Lethou in the Channel Islands, has come up for sale by private treaty now that its present owner, Group Captain William Hedley Cliff, is forced to sell it due to '*private and personal reasons.*'

The island, just two miles off Guernsey has been open as a holiday resort with boats bringing over 6,000 tourists a year and is equipped with a bar, gift shop and even Lethou specific stamps. In the garden is a mulberry tree which has withstood Channel gales for more than 200 Years.

AROUND THE WORLD
"Twin Towers"

The US government has unveiled plans to erect two 1,350-foot-high skyscrapers in New York City to be the home of the World Trade Centre.

The buildings, set to be complete in 1970, will dominate the Manhattan skyline and assume the title of world's tallest building(s), taking over from the Empire State Building. The 110-story building will cost just shy of $350 million and will contain a mixture of offices, exhibition halls, shops, restaurants and a 250-room hotel. The car park will be able to accommodate 1,600 vehicles at once.

THE RACING CAR SHOW

The World Championship winning Lotus 25

Fast cars dating from as early as 1899 right up to modern speed machines were on show for the hundreds of motoring enthusiasts who descended upon the Racing Car Show at Olympia. The event, likely to make even the more regular saloon-car driver giddy, is in just its fifth year of running, but nonetheless has amassed some of the fastest machines man has ever created. The centrepiece of the exhibition is Jim Clark's world championship winning Lotus 25, which steamed its way to the 1963 Formula One World Championship. The programme described the creation of Colin Chapman's motoring genius as *'an innocuous little green and yellow car'* somewhat downplaying its revolutionary nature. Formula One fans gathered in their masses to discuss the ongoing championship in the hope that Clark and Lotus will be able to repeat their championship victory this year.

The 'Racing Through the Years' section also proved to be popular with petrol heads, who marvelled at how far the automotive industry has come since the Cannstatt Daimler race car from 1899. The car on display was raced for three years by a Russian count, and its four cylinder, 1,250 cc engine was the revolution of the age in motor racing. Many people were seemingly very interested in the *'hotted-up'* contemporary saloon cars, named 'touring cars', which were modified versions of many driveway classics. These machines were taken racing by their various manufacturers at speeds of up to 120mph. The dragsters also filled the exhibition hall, the craze having made the trip across the pond from its home in America. These high-powered sprinting machines are capable of doing the quarter mile drag strip in just 8 seconds reaching speeds of 178mph.

Jan 29th - Feb 4th 1964

IN THE NEWS

Wednesday 29 — "US - Soviet Tensions" More disputes have arisen between Russia and the US following the shooting down of an unarmed US training jet that had 'mistakenly' flown into East German airspace.

Thursday 30 — "Meat Famine" Over six million people across two million homes have been left meatless following a workers strike that put a halt to the cattle market in Birmingham. The market closed after 70 slaughter men walked out in sympathy with the 120 meat porters already on strike.

Friday 31 — "TV Satellite" The US Ranger 6 satellite, sent to the moon carrying six television cameras designed to take over 3,000 pictures of the moon's surface, has been revealed to be on the wrong course. Luckily, the direction can be altered from the ground.

Sat 1 Feb — "Cyprus Scare" Peace in Cyprus came perilously close to being broken after Cypriot delegates rejected Britain's proposal for a NATO manned police force for the island.

Sunday 2 — "Bulls Eye on the Moon" After a three-day voyage, the US space craft Ranger 6 has hit the moon but failed to deliver the intended photographs. However, the craft crashed with minute precision on its intended target over 240,000 miles away.

Monday 3 — "Tipping to Go" Tipping on cruise ships is to be replaced by a preliminary surcharge to try to avoid the ongoing loss of sea goers to airlines - where tipping is explicitly forbidden.

Tuesday 4 — "The Queen Mother 'Not Seriously Ill'" After being rushed to hospital and forced to cancel her visit to Canada, New Zealand and Australia, the Queen Mother is to have an emergency operation for appendicitis and is described to be 'not seriously ill'.

HERE IN BRITAIN

"Premium Petrol Scam"

According to a review of over 35 different types of petrol tested by the Consumers' Association, there is next to no difference in filling up your car with more expensive petrol than required. The most cost efficient to performance ratio comes from the bare minimum fuel that will '*not knock your car*'.

The Association did extensive testing in areas of consumption, acceleration, engine cleanliness and engine response, which proved the negligible difference not only between grades of petrol, but also between brands. No '*best buy*' brand of petrol was named.

AROUND THE WORLD

"Kafka in Moscow"

For the first time since the Russian Revolution in 1917, the writings of banned Western authors have been permitted to be published in the country again.

In response to international claims that Russia was adopting a 'cultural isolationism', writers banned under Stalin, and including Franz Kafka, Proust and Joyce, have been published, with a typical communist spin; Kafka is claimed to have been a '*pessimistic victim of the Capitalist environment*'. It is thought that the younger Russian generation is completely ignorant of these classical writers.

No Tugs For Queen

The Queen Elizabeth leaving Southampton (main) and arriving in New York (inset)

The RMS Queen Elizabeth liner has collided with a pier in New York City after making a first attempt to dock without the aid of tugs. The tugboat, tanker and barge workers in the US port are on strike over a pay dispute and it is not known when they will return to work. After colliding with the pier, the ship was successfully attached on the second try, with only minimal and cosmetic damage to the structure of the vessel.

Although a number of windows were broken during the operation, Commodore F. Watts - who was adept at docking the Queen Mary without tugs - had an added complication as the Queen Elizabeth was berthed for the first time at a new pier, the Cunard company recently having moved its large liner terminal from Pier 90 to Pier 92. At first it was thought that the ship should be diverted to safeguard the lives of the 1,000 passengers on board, but Commodore Watts assured the owners it could be done. Another ship, the Italian liner Cristoforo Colombo, was not so successful and two steel girders were damaged when she collided with the upper deck of a pier on the Hudson river.

The RMS Queen Elizabeth provided a luxury liner service between Southampton and New York and was the largest liner afloat, a title which remained for 56 years after she was built. Her sister ship, the Queen Mary, was built first and the Queen Elizabeth was 12 feet longer with an improved design. The ship was launched in 1938, and was named after the then Queen Elizabeth, soon to become the Queen Mother, and had served as a troopship during the Second World War, before assuming her intended role as a luxury liner in 1946.

FEBRUARY 5TH - 11TH 1964

IN THE NEWS

Wednesday 5 — **"Amphibious Cars"** Britain has placed an order for 50 amphibious cars from West Germany. These can not only act as transport on road and on water but can also link together to form a bridge or ferry.

Thursday 6 — **"Railways Under the Channel"** 1970 is the date set by British and French authorities to begin work on an undersea rail tunnel spanning the length of the English Channel. The project is estimated to cost around £160M.

Friday 7 — **"Beatlemania in the USA"** The British hit band, the Beatles, has arrived in New York at the start of their first tour of the United States. They were greeted by over 3,000 American fans, many of whom had skipped school or work.

Saturday 8 — **"Firebombed Theatre"** The Rainbow Theatre situated on the southern Blackpool pier has gone up in flames. Hundreds of people lined the promenade to watch the 50-foot flames which could be seen up to ten miles away.

Sunday 9 — **"Ex-PM To Not Seek Re-election"** Harold Macmillan has announced that he will not stand for re-election in the upcoming General Election. After resigning from Number 10 last winter, Mr Macmillan ends his 40-year long career in politics.

Monday 10 — **"Australian Naval Collision"** It is suspected that at least 103 people have died following the sinking of the Australian destroyer 'Voyager' which collided with the aircraft carrier 'Melbourne' off the coast of New South Wales.

Tuesday 11 — **"Fanny Hill Memoirs"** The 18th century novel 'Fanny Hill, Memoirs of a Woman of Pleasure' by John Cleland, has been ruled by magistrates to be obscene and all copies of the book have been demanded to be forfeited.

HERE IN BRITAIN

"Warning Of Warning Signs"

A trial on the M5 of an illuminated warning sign is set to be implemented in the coming months. Currently, the hazards to be indicated will be: 'Slow', 'Accident', 'Fog' or 'Skid Risk'. This first sign will be manually operated and its visibility assessed in fog, bright sunlight and at night.

The Ministry says that, to gain maximum experience as quickly as possible, the warning may appear even when no special hazard exists, but motorists will receive advance notices of the trials. Public feedback will determine if the experiment is be deemed successful.

AROUND THE WORLD

"German Carnival Prerogative"

The Roman Catholic areas of Germany held their annual carnival with Dusseldorf, Mainz, Munich and Cologne amongst major cities holding large celebrations, and major public figures being the 'butts' of their humour. In Cologne alone, 28 floats, 62 bands, 300 horses and 3,000 'fools' processed through the streets, with the highlight being the float of the Minister of the Interior, Herr Hocherl, who was portrayed on the phone with foamy liquid pouring from the receiver. The Minister's officials had been caught 'accidentally' tapping the phone lines of a German Brewery.

THE BEATLES ARE HARMLESS

The Beatles arriving in New York (main) and on a TV show (inset)

"*Beatle Bedded by a Bug*" was one headline run by an American newspaper amidst the 'Beatlemania' sweeping across the United States at the outset of the band's first USA tour. George Harrison made the front page after catching a minor cold and having to take to his bed ahead of an evening performance. All across New York, teenagers can be seen wearing mop-headed wigs, not having time to grow their own hair to a suitable length. Thousands flocked to the airport to see the band arrive from England.

Many have called the band, '*the most profitable British export of the time*', with sell out concerts planned all through their tour. Nevertheless, even with their newfound American fame, there was a large degree of hotel confusion upon arriving in New York. The hotel management claims to have not been aware of the coming stars, and instead assumed they were mere British businessmen! People have since been requested to remove their wigs before entering the hotel dining room, and the poor hotel lounge musician has been forced to decline requests for Beatle's songs in the lobby due to them being '*not suitable for the violin*'. However, the fears of an uncontrollable American teenage craze were put to bed after the band's first television performance, watched by thousands of the American public. '*The Beatles are Harmless*' read one American newspaper headline, after the modest and agreeable performance by the band relieved much of the United States population, who have been outraged at the overt sexuality of performers like Elvis.

According to some reports, given the current tensions between England and the US over the British sale of buses to Cuba, the Beatles touring America may help to patch much of the animosity between our countries.

February 12th - 18th 1964

IN THE NEWS

Wednesday 12 — "Gambling Profits May be Taxed" The government is considering a new tax on all forms of gambling as over £10m a year net profit is made by Britain's 'one-armed bandits'

Thursday 13 — "Flying Boats" Three 140-ton Princess flying boats have been sold to a company in the Bahamas, for conversion into US space component carriers. They will become the largest operational aircraft in the world.

Friday 14 — "Female Engineer Charter" The Confederation of Shipbuilding and Engineering Unions have received a demand for equal pay for the 500,000 women in the industry.

Saturday 15 — "M6 Joint Traffic Command" Three police forces have joined together to patrol the M6 motorway by cars and a helicopter.

Sunday 16 — "More Warships to the Scrapyard" A further 23 naval vessels have been decommissioned by the Royal Navy and sent to be broken down for parts. The total number of ships scrapped in the last four years has reached 93.

Monday 17 — "Ford Redundancy Fears" Ford Motor Company have warned workers at their Dagenham plant that they may face redundancy at some point in the coming weeks. The issue stems from the increased purchase tax in the government's recent budget.

Tuesday 18 — "6 Mile Taxi Fares to go" The Government has conceded that the current limit for London Taxis is too low, and it is likely to be raised to 10 miles. Since the days of horse-drawn cabs no driver has been compelled to take a passenger more than six miles 'on the clock'. Beyond that distance he may bargain with the hirer about the fare.

HERE IN BRITAIN

"Northern Writers on Radio"

Ten plays written by northern authors *'without a mill, fish and chip shop, or cobbles in any of them'* have been commissioned by the BBC to be broadcast live over the next few months as part of their ongoing 'talent encouragement project'.

The plays have been named 'the Northern Wave' and a collection of poems by northern writers, 'the Northern Drift'. Nevertheless, following the publishing of the itinerary, the public response hasn't been all good, with one person remarking that the titles of the collections *'remind him more of fishing boats than literary endeavours.'*

AROUND THE WORLD

"China to Have Last Million Words"

China keeps detailed government records on the perceived wrongs done to them by other nations. The current tally against American intervention and imposition into Chinese waters or airspace sits at 276, and the Russians fare little better, with thousands of pages of documents recording multiple references to slights of China in both the national and provincial Soviet press - criticism which the Chinese do not take lightly.

They add that *'in accordance with the principle of equality among fraternal parties the Chinese side has the right to publish a commensurate number of replies.'*

VALENTINE'S DAY

Victorian Valentine's Day cards

Since the end of the Second World War, Europe has seen a return to the custom of romantic and charming Valentine's Day festivities, with a rapid rise in consumerism, and American influence, in the commercialisation of the day. British love makers flock to card and chocolate shops to buy gifts for their loved ones as the country gets swept up with the air of love.

The Valentine's Day festival itself is somewhat mysterious in origin, with multiple different sources offering multiple different views. The trail goes back to the Saint Valentine, or one of three possible Saint Valentines, all of whom were martyred. The most recognised saint of the three, defied the Roman Emperor Claudius after he outlawed marriage for young men, by continuing to perform marriage ceremonies for young lovers in the street. He was beheaded for his treason. Others suggest that Saint Valentine was a Bishop also beheaded by Claudius and the third, a Valentine killed for helping Christians escape the cruelty of Roman prisons. According to one legend, an imprisoned Valentine sent the first 'Valentine greeting' to a young girl he had fallen in love with, possibly his captor's daughter, and he signed his letter *'from your Valentine'* - an expression still used to this day.

The festival itself, nevertheless, acts as a celebration of the life of Saint Valentine, possibly all three Saint Valentines, but wasn't an overtly romantic celebration until characterised as such by Geoffrey Chaucer in his 1375 poem, *'For this was sent on Seynt Valentine's day ... when every foul cometh ther to choose his mate'.* The oldest known valentine was a poem written in 1415 by Charles, Duke of Orleans, to his wife while he was imprisoned in the Tower of London following his capture at the Battle of Agincourt.

February 19th – 25th 1964

IN THE NEWS

Wednesday 19 — **"Battle of the Chancellors"** The scheduled TV debate between the Chancellor of the Exchequer and his opposition counterpart has been abandoned after Mr Maudling, the current Chancellor, requested *'more time to fit the confrontation into his schedule'*.

Thursday 20 — **"The New £10 Note"** After being absent for 19 years, the £10 note will return to British currency and bears a portrait of the Queens head. After ceasing to be legal tender in 1945, the note is being reintroduced following the success of the £5.

Friday 21 — **"Flaming Pencil Too Costly"** Plans for the British T188 Aircraft, nicknamed the 'Flaming Pencil', designed ten years ago as a high-speed plane capable of speeds up to 2,000 mph, have been abandoned.

Saturday 22 — **"Postman Strike"** Following the refusal of Postmaster General Mr Bevins to agree to a requested pay increase for the job, 120,000 postmen across the country are threatening a 'go slow' or to strike for the first time since 1891.

Sunday 23 — **"Electric Revolution"** A brand new, four seat, electric car, capable of speeds up to 35 mph and to drive 50 miles for 1s 6d (8p), is to make its debut. Recharging takes 10 hours, and the car will cost no more than its petrol counterpart.

Monday 24 — **"Britain Recognises Zanzibar"** After the expulsion of the British High Commissioner and exile of the Sultan, the British Government has decided to officially recognise the new government and President of Zanzibar.

Tuesday 25 — **"Cassius Clay Champion of the World"** In the biggest boxing upset in many years, Cassius Clay defeated Sonny Liston in just six rounds to assume the title of Heavyweight Champion of the World.

HERE IN BRITAIN

"Too Tall"

The plans for a Mosque in Regents Park have run into complications following the revelation that the building would contravene a five-year-old stipulation that no high building should be erected at the edge of Regents Park.

The land for the Mosque was gifted to the Central London Mosque Trust by George VI in 1944, but it was only last January that the plans for the building were released. Alternative sites are being considered, along with possible alterations to the original designs to accommodate the surroundings.

AROUND THE WORLD

"Life Jacket for Venus"

The famous Venus de Milo is travelling by cargo vessel from Marseilles to Japan, where it is on loan for an exhibition in Tokyo and Kyoto. Unlike the Mona Lisa, which made the trip from France to America in a luxury state room on the liner 'France', the marble Venus de Milo statue is travelling upright in the hold in a special crate surrounded by asbestos, whilst wearing an outsize life jacket in case of shipwreck. She will be guarded by a number of French police officers on the month-long trip to Japan.

YOUR COUNTRY NEEDS YOU

THE ARMY OF TODAY'S ALL RIGHT!

This is the Army: THE LIFE FOR A MAN OF ACTION

Army Outward Bound School 1963

In December last year, the strength of the British Army fell by over 450 men and there are calls for improvement in marketing the armed forces to appeal to young people, giving a new and impressive picture of the military profession with the adverts showing the variety of experience and responsibility which face a young officer and the technical and academic challenges of service life.

Previous advertising has concentrated on the life of the Sandhurst cadet and it is clear that in the minds of many people, the profession consists principally of mentally enclosed buffoons who converse in sharp monosyllables and live exclusively on a diet of port. This is partly a result of some of the curiously stylised portraits which appear in certain television programmes where Army officers tend to wear their badges of rank upside down and get old-fashioned 'swagger sticks' caught between their legs. While the War Office do not deny that there are still officers whose intellectual gifts are minimal, in general the requirement for intelligence, enterprise and professional competence compares favourably with those of other professions.

At the same time, a symbol is needed to identify this new Army. The Navy's aircraft carrier and the V bombers of the Royal Air Force are vivid images, but for the Army, tanks, rifles and bayonets, however modern, are too evocative of past wars. Last year's advertising campaign brought it somewhat up to date with a picture of a member of the Army's Outward Bound School negotiating a precipice in North Wales also stating that one of the attractions of the school is a *'6.45 am dip in the Irish Sea every morning'* - a prospect which many officers thought was carrying image-making a shade too far.

FEB 26TH - MARCH 3RD 1964

IN THE NEWS

Wednesday 26 — **"Keel for Polaris"** The first major step in the production of British Polaris submarines has been taken, with the keel of the first submarine, named HMS Resolution, being laid at the shipyard of Vickers Armstrong's Ltd.

Thursday 27 — **"Queen to Quebec?"** The Premier of Quebec has assured the British Royal Family that maximum protection will be allocated for the Queen on her upcoming visit, after a leader from one of the countries' terror groups warned the Queen to stay away.

Friday 28 — **"Man or Beast"** A young British biologist working in Washington believes that following her extensive study of Chimpanzees over the last three years, the Scientific world should 're-evaluate' the definition of a human.

Saturday 29 — **"Hovercraft to France"** Westland Aircraft, the company responsible for the production of the world's first hovercraft, believe that they have successfully designed a vessel capable of operating as a regular ferry service across the English Channel.

Sun 1 March — **"Air Crash Catastrophe"** 75 British holidaymakers and eight crew have been confirmed dead after a Britannia aircraft crashed into an Austrian peak. The plane lost contact over the mountain region yesterday.

Monday 2 — **"Fishy Business"** Fourteen of the sixteen countries in attendance at The European Fisheries Conference have agreed on a new six-mile limit for fishing off a country's coast and a further six mile 'belt' for exclusive fishing rights.

Tuesday 3 — **"Car Production Halted"** Over 11,000 British Motor Corporation employees lay idle as ongoing strikes put a halt to the production lines of Morris' and Mini's across Midland factories, it is thought that BMC Rover employees will soon follow suit.

HERE IN BRITAIN
"Winkle Picker Adventurers"

Three boys on an adventure scheme in the Lake District were turned back from the higher fells as they had 'inappropriate equipment'. One wore 'Winkle Picker' shoes, one gym trainers, and the other his sister's boots.

The rise in popularity of adventure schemes and awards has coincided with the rise in avoidable incidents and last year, 13 people just 'fell off' the rocks and one woman got a knee jammed in a crack, taking a rescue team six hours to release her, using half a pound of butter and two tins of sardines.

AROUND THE WORLD
"Car Trouble"

New York City Council have reported over 2,600 cars have been abandoned on the streets of the city since the beginning of the year, a figure considerably up from previous reports.

Although acute, the issue usually occurs in the early months of a calendar year due to the large number of cars registered and insured during this time. Just 19 owners have used the proper channels, contacting the Department of Sanitation to dispose of their unwanted vehicles, a fact which the Commissioner of Sanitation is 'disappointed' about.

Supersonic RAF

The RAF Vulcan was a long range, high altitude bomber that was in service from 1956 to 1984

The RAF's supersonic, low level 'TSR2 Bomber' aircraft is expected to come into commission this summer, somewhat later than previously planned. Also more expensive than originally thought, at £500 million, the new stealth aircraft is capable of incredible low-level penetration to such an extent that they will *'skim the ground'*. The machines are hailed by the RAF chiefs as *'one of the most potent and flexible instruments of military power yet devised'* and 30 more have been ordered on top of the original 20 development aircraft. *(Editor's Note: Only one TSR2 ever flew due to rising costs and test flight issues).*

The RAF itself was formed at a critical period of the First World War, by the amalgamation of the Army's and Navy's flying wings, the Royal Flying Corps and the Royal Naval Air Service. When the war of 1914 started, the aeroplane was a new and untried weapon, strictly limited in its uses and not sure of its role. Rapidly it developed both as a weapon of offence and defence and the RAF was born after three years and eight months of conflict. When the allies mounted their counter-offensive in 1918, the RAF was able to concentrate 1,290 first-line aircraft against its opponents' 340, and, enjoying this air superiority, was able to disrupt the Germans' communications and harass their troops by low flying attacks.

When the Armistice came, the RAF was the greatest air force in the world, both numerically and in quality of equipment, possessing more than 200 squadrons, 22,647 aircraft of all, 103 airships and a total strength of 291,000 officers and men. After the war the Service shrank to a shadow of its former self but managed to keep many members possessing a pioneering spirit, which in turn, maintained the high standards and increased the prestige of British aviation throughout the world.

March 4th – 10th 1964

IN THE NEWS

Wednesday 4 — **"Judge and Jury"** The district court in Dallas has at last formed a jury to hear the case against Jack Ruby. The eleventh and twelfth jurors were sworn in after a total of 162 candidates had been examined during the first 14 days of the trial.

Thursday 5 — **"Crushing Casualties"** Over 100 people were injured in or around the Manchester United vs Sunderland FA Cup match at Roker Park football ground, after 70,000 people were let in to the 62,000-capacity stadium and a further 40,000 congregated outside.

Friday 6 — **"Moving Bank Holiday"** The Government has announced their plans to trial moving the August Bank Holiday to the last Monday of the month in both 1965 and 1966.

Saturday 7 — **"Olympic Grant"** The Minister with a special responsibility for sport, announced a state grant would be made available for the athletes competing in the British Olympic Team at the Tokyo Games next October.

Sunday 8 — **"Doping Shock"** After a shock revelation, stewards are investigating the doping of one of the nation's favourite hurdling racehorses, Antiar. Antiar's trainer, Major Peter Cazalet, also trains horses for the Queen Mother.

Monday 9 — **"In an Alarming State"** Ahead of its 800th Birthday, Bristol Cathedral is launching an appeal for £300,000 to be put towards vital restoration work. The current state of the building is described as 'alarming'.

Tuesday 10 — **"It's a Boy"** It was announced today that the Queen has safely given birth to her fourth child and third son. Both mother and baby are happy and healthy. The boy will be third in line to the throne, ahead of Princess Anne.

HERE IN BRITAIN

"To the Stocks"

The MP for Middleton and Prestwich has requested that the 1625 Sunday Observance Act be repealed, after members of a bowling club were threatened with 'three hours in the stocks'.

Police were called to the club the day before one of the groups' fortnightly Sunday handicaps, where they warned the members that if the game went ahead, a three-shilling fine or three hours in the stocks would be the punishment. The ancient law prohibits *'meetings of people outside their own parish on the Lord's Day for any sport or pastime whatsoever'*.

AROUND THE WORLD

"Battle of the Bronze Door"

The residents of the small town of Monte Sant Angelo near Foggia in Italy physically prevented the removal of the bronze doors of their Basilica, intended for an upcoming international exhibition of Byzantine art in Athens.

Groups of peasants guarded the doors throughout the night and were joined in the day by school children who refused to attend their lessons. The doors date from as early as 1076 and were a gift to the sanctuary, built over the spot where the Archangel Michael is said to have made an appearance in the Fifth Century.

IDEAL HOME EXHIBITION

The Ideal Home Show included new household appliances and new home designs

The Ideal Home Exhibition 1964 has been met with mixed reviews from critics and the public alike, because of its 'forward thinking' and 'futuristic' attitude towards home furnishings. The preview house, built by the British Aluminium Company, looks *'almost traditional'* but was nonetheless filled with items that can easily be churned out on a production line. The exhibition is promoting a new *'catalogue shopping'* slant on home furnishing, with members of the public able to look 'room by room' at exactly how they want their homes to look. The Ministry of Housing's 5M 'flexible 'house' shows the new attitude towards home owning, as expansion and building is becoming quicker, easier and more efficient. 'Flexible housing' as it has been named, is estimated to cost around £3,000 for the average 5–6-person family and can even include features such as a 'round kitchen' - much to the bewilderment of many critics but the designer said *'the gentle curve gives a new dimensional element'*.

When the Lord Mayor of London rode in state with his sheriffs and aldermen through the streets of London on an October morning in 1908, he was going to Olympia to open the first Ideal Home Exhibition. Promoted by the proprietor of the Daily Mail, it was to be 'a demonstration of the best and latest products for the home maker.' It had taken eight days to build and attracted less than 400 exhibitors. Visitors would have seen many new ideas and products. The latest brands of blacking for the iron kitchen grate and whitening for the doorstep; new copper pans, heated from underneath by coal fires, in which the housewife – or her servant – could boil the laundry and a mangle with which to wring it. Gentlemen would find pomade for waxing a moustache and ladies, silk-painted fire screens.

March 11th - 17th 1964

IN THE NEWS

Wednesday 11 — "**Underwater Music**" The new Charles Forte Airport Hotel, directly opposite London Airport, houses a swimming pool not only equipped with underwater lighting, but also an underwater sound system too.

Thursday 12 — "**Trident Makes Flight**" The replacement for the British European Airways Service's Comet aircraft has made its first voyage. The 600 mph Trident, carrying 79 passengers, made the first trip between London and Copenhagen.

Friday 13 — "**Good Small Shops**" *'Good small shops will survive'* is the word from the Chairman of the Consumer Council following what she deemed as *'unnecessary'* agitation after the government's Resale Prices Bill earlier this year.

Saturday 14 — "**Ruby to Death**" Jack Ruby has officially been sentenced to death by electric chair having been found guilty of the murder of Lee Harvey Oswald, the alleged assassin of President John F Kennedy. Ruby's legal team have appealed the decision.

Sunday 15 — "**Liz Says 'I Do'**" Richard Burton and Elizabeth Taylor were married in Montreal's Church of the Messiah, Canada. The couple had made a secret flight from Toronto where Burton is playing the lead role in 'Hamlet'.

Monday 16 — "**US Airbase to Go**" The United States Navy is giving up their air station at Malling in Kent and transferring to the USAF base in Suffolk. The Kent location will go back to being an RAF fighter base, as it was during the Second World War.

Tuesday 17 — "**Britain's Better Missile**" The Polaris Missiles commissioned by the Royal Navy to be housed in its new fleet of submarines, will have a 60% longer range, but be no larger than the ones currently used by the US Armed Forces.

HERE IN BRITAIN

"The Royal Baby"

Princess Margaret and the Queen Mother were the first of the extended Royal family to visit the Queen and her new-born son at Buckingham Palace. The pair arrived in the same car and stayed at the Palace for over 30 minutes. Flags were flown on public buildings and over the palace flew the ceremonial standard.

Royal salutes were fired in London, Windsor, Edinburgh and Sterling; Lightning fighters of the RAF staged a flypast over the centre of London and in ships and naval establishments throughout the world, the order to 'splice the mainbrace' was carried out.

AROUND THE WORLD

"No Daffodil on the Coin"

In Canada, patriotic fervour has been aroused by the omission of the daffodil from the design of the newly minted silver dollar commemorating the visit of the Fathers of Confederation to Charlottetown and Quebec City in 1864.

The coin contains the French fleurs-de-lys, the English rose, the Scottish thistle and the Irish Shamrock, but a Welsh reference is conspicuously absent. If no daffodil is added to a second minting, Mr Pearson, the PM is unlikely to find 'a welcome in the valley' next time he visits Harlech!

Unlucky For Some!

This ship has no deck 13.

XIII DEATH

LA MORT

A court ruling by the Queen's Bench on Friday 13th determined that a stake of more than 6d at a time on a fruit machine was to be illegal. A London Club owner had appealed against a charge of contravening the Betting and Gambling Act by installing a new type of fruit machine allowing stakes of up to 2s 6d, but came up short when gambling with the courts on this auspicious day.

For many, Friday 13th is regarded as a most unlucky day. Superstitions surrounding the date are thought to originate in the middle-ages and there are dozens of fears, myths and old wives' tales associated with the date all over the world.

The number 13 and Friday both have an individual long history of bringing bad luck. In the Bible, Judas, who betrayed Jesus, was the 13th guest to sit down to the Last Supper. In Norse mythology, a dinner party of the gods was ruined by the 13th guest called Loki, 'god of deceit and evil', who caused the world to be plunged into darkness. Peoples of the Mediterranean, regarded 13 with suspicion, not being as perfect as 12, which is divisible in many ways.

As for 'Friday', according to tradition, Adam and Eve were expelled from Eden; Cain murdered Abel; St John the Baptist was beheaded the enactment of the order of Herod for the massacre of the innocents, all took place on a Friday. In Chaucer's Canterbury Tales, written in the 14th Century, he says 'and on a Friday fell all this mischance'. Here in Britain, Friday was once known as 'Hangman's Day' because it was usually when people who had been condemned to death would be hanged and the great crash of 1869, when the price of gold plummeted, was on Friday too.

March 18th – 24th 1964

IN THE NEWS

Wednesday 18 — **"Homes for Former Prisoners"** The St Leonard's Housing Association has revealed plans for a scheme to house former prisoners involving converting properties into self-contained flats. Of the 2,000 men released from London prisons last year, it is thought that over two thirds are homeless.

Thursday 19 — **"More Power"** Plans for a new power station to be built on the banks of the Yorkshire Ouse have been published. The site will be Britain's and Europe's biggest, capable of 3,000 megawatts; the project will cost £105 million.

Friday 20 — **"Vauxhall Expansion"** Vauxhall Motors announced plans to expand their British manufacturing with a new factory in Ellesmere Port, costing around £30 million.

Saturday 21 — **"Pocket Radio"** In an attempt to return the role of the 'bobby on the beat' police officer to its previous importance, a new battery powered handheld transistor radio has been put into operation by the Durham Police Force.

Sunday 22 — **"Venus de Milo Safe"** The Venus de Milo statue has been delivered successfully to Japan after a month-long journey from France. It will be on exhibition in Tokyo and Kyoto. The artwork was slightly damaged with a small fragment of the original marble breaking off.

Monday 23 — **"Hospitals Call on Army"** Ahead of expected power cuts arising from the government's ban of overtime imposed on manual labourers, hospitals have been forced to call on the army to provide power generators.

Tuesday 24 — **"Four More Concordes"** The Australian national airline, Qantas, have ordered four of the Anglo-French Concorde Airliners, costing around £3.5 million each. The total number of aircraft orders now exceed 40 as business booms for the supersonic aircraft.

HERE IN BRITAIN
"The Alphabet"

Having been introduced three years ago, the use of a simplified alphabet to help teach young children how to read has come back as largely successful. The initial teaching alphabet (ITA) was devised by Sir James Pitman, a grandson of the shorthand inventor.

It is a 44-character alphabet, with each sound represented by one symbol, and the educationists who are supporting the new method say that children, 8,000 - 10,000 in the last three years, who learn to read this way will be able to transfer to reading the ordinary alphabet without difficulty.

AROUND THE WORLD
"Battle of the Tins"

The U.S. Government, and in particular the Department of Agriculture, is in the middle of a 'chicken soup war' over how much meat there should be in a tin of chicken soup.

Although the whole chicken soup industry is under scrutiny, the focus is placed on the 'chicken noodle soup'. Under the law, a tin of 'wet' or liquid chicken noodle soup must contain at least 2% by weight of chicken meat but there is a loophole in the law which does not demand the same minimum standard in a tin or packet of dehydrated soup.

GREAT ST BERNARD TUNNEL

The entrance to the tunnel (inset) which is the only road open in winter between the Aosta valley in Italy and France. The snow covered Grand St Bernard Pass (main picture) is closed October to June

The first ever road tunnel under the Alps was opened in majestic fashion with flags and a ceremony, as five British cars became the first motor vehicles to drive the passage. Having been flown to Geneva, the cars were driven through treacherous conditions and heavy snowfall, reaching speeds of up to 90mph, with a Swiss police escort, in order to reach the tunnel by the scheduled opening time of 8am. The cars triumphantly made it, and it was reported that the only disappointment was the lack of Swiss girls in national costume who were meant to draw lots to see which of the cars would go through the tunnel first. It was rumoured that the conditions got too much for them, so they instead returned home.

Britain was chosen as a suitable host country for the first motor vehicles to pass through because of our great tourist potential, thus a Hillman Imp led a Triumph 2000, a Ford Zephyr, and a Sunbeam Alpine through the tunnel and onto the Mediterranean coast, where they met a contingent of Italian Fiats who were doing the journey in reverse. The aim of the trip was to prove that the journey between London and Genoa could now be done by car in less than 12 hours.

The St Bernard Tunnel is 3.6 miles long, and the roads either side are protected by nine miles of covered galleries to ensure dry and safe roads at all times of year. The name of the tunnel comes directly from the Grand St. Bernard Pass and indirectly from the saint who in AD 1049 founded the hospice high above the tunnel at the summit of the pass. In days gone by, the monks of the hospice used their large St. Bernard dogs to help rescue stranded travellers.

March 25th – 31st 1964

IN THE NEWS

Wednesday 25 — **"London Stansted"** The £10 million site for London's third airport has been picked as Stansted in Essex, 36 miles outside the city by road. Over 100 possible sites were reviewed before the decision was made.

Thursday 26 — **"Great Train Robbery"** After considering their verdicts in secret for 65 hours, the jury for the 'great train robbery' trial found seven men guilty of the theft of over £2 million, and a further nine on charges of conspiracy.

Friday 27 — **"Earthquake State"** Alaska has been hit with earthquakes so strong that the tremors have being felt as far away as New Zealand.

Saturday 28 — **"Quebec not Sydney"** Soviet Satellite Cosmos 23 has re-entered the atmosphere above North America, with debris falling on Quebec as the space vessel broke up. There were some red faces for those who predicted it would fall on Sydney, Australia.

Sunday 29 — **"Clacton Rowdyism"** Over 97, mainly young, people have been arrested by Clacton police after disturbances and fights emerged in the town and on the seafront over the weekend. Many of the youths were openly hostile towards the police.

Monday 30 — **"Empty Easter Beaches"** Beaches have been left deserted and traffic on the roads was very light, as the country experienced the coldest Easter holiday for 30 years. However, road accidents and fatalities were higher than previous years.

Tuesday 31 — **"Pirate Radio"** A transmitting radio station calling itself 'Radio Caroline' has begun broadcasting off the coast of Felixstowe in Suffolk, disrupting ship to shore communications. The broadcasting vessel is outside British territorial waters therefore the government is powerless to stop the transmission.

HERE IN BRITAIN

"JFK Memorials"

The British memorial to former U.S. President John F Kennedy will take two forms. The government has approved a monument on an acre of land at Runnymede, the land being given in perpetuity to the United States.
The second, intangible element, will be a scholarship fund to send British undergraduates to study at the Massachusetts Institute of Technology to further the President's interest in bringing together, into 'a fruitful combination', traditional humane studies and modern technology in the direction of world affairs.

AROUND THE WORLD

"Silver Dollar Rush"

Hundreds of Americans, some of whom had camped on the pavement all night, lined the streets outside the US Treasury building anxious to exchange their dollar bills for silver coins.
Many exchanged hundreds of dollar bills and staggered under the weight of bags of silver, some used wheelbarrows. The rush was caused by the discovery of millions of 1880 'Morgan dollar coins' each of which could be worth between $10 and $30. People hope they can receive one in exchange for their dollar bills.

MAUNDY MONEY

The Royal Maundy ceremony of 1877

Following the birth of her third son earlier this month, the Queen was not present at the Maundy Service in Westminster Abbey this week. Princess Mary, the Princess Royal, who is the Queen's aunt, took her place and distributed the Royal Maundy in the traditional ceremony.

The distribution of Maundy Money, which takes place on the Thursday before Easter, is the modern development of an ancient ceremony said to be derived from when Christ washed his disciples' feet the evening before his crucifixion. In Britain the service goes back many centuries and Elizabeth I personally took part in 1572, in the hall at Greenwich. On that occasion a laundress, the sub-Almoner and the Lord High Almoner washed the feet of the poor people, and the feet then being, apparently, thoroughly clean, were again washed and kissed by the Queen herself. She then distributed broadcloth for the making of clothes and fish, bread and wine. Royalty continued to take part but the last time the foot-washing ritual took place was in 1685.

For many years the ceremony took place in Whitehall Chapel moving later to Westminster Abbey. The Queen, accompanied by the Duke of Edinburgh, has personally distributed her royal gift almost every year since her coronation, and will undoubtedly be disappointed to miss this year's ceremony. In addition to banknotes and cash which have now taken the place of all other forms of gift, the pensioners receive some of the world's most interesting coins presented in a small leather purse, with as many pence as the monarch has years of age. The recipients themselves number as many men and as many women as the monarch has years. The coins are still, today, struck in silver and polished like proof coins.

April 1ST - 7TH 1964

IN THE NEWS

Wednesday 1   **"Junction Boxes"** The aims of the 'junction box' traffic control is that there should never be stationary vehicles holding up other traffic in a box marked by criss-cross yellow lines at street crossings. In a trial of six on London's West End roads, the police gave a 'negative' report – *'not much congestion yet.'*

Thursday 2   **"Smoking Bus"** Manchester has become the first UK city to ban smoking totally on public buses. Previously it was banned on lower decks but passengers sometimes had to go upstairs to a smoky atmosphere.

Friday 3   **"Purple Hearts"** The police hope to gain increased powers to punish those found in possession of the 'pep pills' following the Drugs (Prevention of Misuse) Bill becoming law. Rising crime in youths is being linked to 'purple heart' consumption.

Saturday 4   **"Washington to London"** TWA, one of the premier American airlines, is to introduce a non-stop, seven-hour flight from Washington DC to London and will increase the daily number of flights to Britain from two to three.

Sunday 5   **"Seat Belt Success"** Information from over 800 crashes show that wearing a seat belt reduces risk in the event of an accident by as much as 80%. At present, between 12% and 16% of cars on British roads have them fitted.

Monday 6   **"News for the Deaf"** BBC 2 is to host a special TV news review broadcast on Sundays, for deaf people. This will involve using sign language and more pictures to aid reporting.

Tuesday 7   **"Pirate Radio"** The Government is considering jamming the signal to try to counter the growing number of pirate radio broadcasts from outside English territorial waters.

HERE IN BRITAIN

"M6 Air Experiment"

Driver's behaviour may soon be recorded by helicopters patrolling the M6 motorway between Preston and Stafford with a joint motorway force of 80 constables, sergeants and inspectors, equipped with patrol cars, motorcycles and a helicopter.

The main purposes are to see what steps can be taken to reduce motorway accidents as well as for spotting and reporting accidents, taking motorway casualties to hospital, giving fog warnings and reporting dangerous driving.

AROUND THE WORLD

"Salad Bowl Comradeship"

Over the last several weeks, the restoration of the Russian equivalent to the English 'Sir' or 'Madam' has been a topic of hot conversation in Moscow. Stories abound on the limitations of the addresses currently permitted. One man described the problem of trying to gain a woman's attention, he had not noted her name, at the dinner table. He felt, *'Would you like some salad, comrade (Tovarich)?'* was too solemn, and *'Citizen (Grazhdanka), take some salad,'* would lack warmth, whereas *'Girl'* could be patronising to 'a mother of five'!

Dartmoor Dodgers

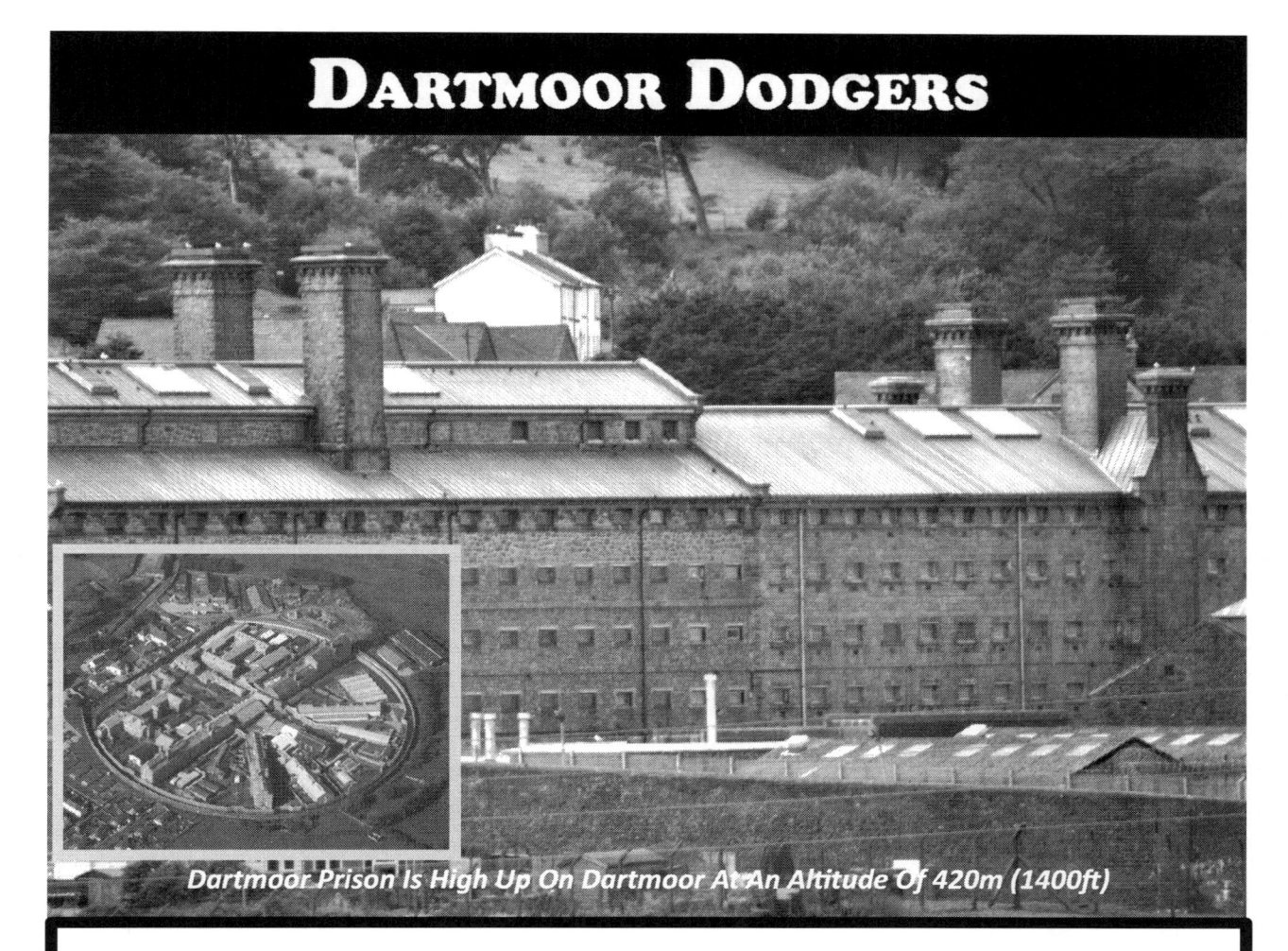

Dartmoor Prison Is High Up On Dartmoor At An Altitude Of 420m (1400ft)

Twenty-seven prisoners have sampled the attraction of freedom found when escaping from Dartmoor prison this year. They have escaped by walking away from a working party to overpowering the driver of a fuel tanker delivering to the prison. But one memorable escape was in 1962.

Albert King wriggled and twisted his way out of the jail and left behind one of the biggest escape puzzles in the prison's history. King, who was serving a twelve-year sentence for safe breaking, dug a hole in the floor of his cell and tunnelled a way to a ventilating shaft leading out to the prison yard.
He put a dummy in his bed to fool prison officers making the regular night check. Then, in his pants and vest and with his body apparently greased, he wriggled through the shaft.
The next stage was to squeeze through a 14in by 10in grille into the yard. He emerged in the darkness of early morning.
The next barrier was the 20ft high outer wall of the jail. Once over that, it is believed that he was picked up by a friend with clothes and a car.
King's getaway was in the pattern of escape which is regarded as a Dartmoor "classic" – that of "Rubber-bones Webb" in 1951 who also dug up his cell floor, left a dummy and wriggled out through a ventilation shaft.

Like Webb, "Corkscrew" King left the jail authorities with some puzzling problems, especially,
• How did he break open the stone floor of his cell without being seen or heard and how did he get rid of the rubble?
• How did he grease his body for the twist through the shaft?
• How did he climb the 20ft high wall? With a ladder like "Rubber Bones Webb"?

April 8th – 14th 1964

IN THE NEWS

Wednesday 8 **"Happy Nurses Mean Quicker Cures"** A study of student nurse wastage has revealed that the happier the nursing staff are, the more efficiently they do their job, and the quicker patients recover.

Thursday 9 **"Overshot Landing"** A US Boeing 707 overran the runway at Kennedy International Airport, New York, plunging into a marshy inlet off Jamaica Bay. Most injuries occurred as people struggled to the shore through waist-high water and mud.

Friday 10 **"Channel Tunnel Reality"** Now that approval has been given for the project, the Government are being quick to approve the first stages of the planned Channel Tunnel between England and France.

Saturday 11 **"University of Warwick"** A detailed panoramic birds eye view model has been created for the planned University of Warwick. The University is to be closely linked with industry and commerce.

Sunday 12 **"Changing Orbit"** On the anniversary of Yuri Gagarin's first flight into space, the Soviet Union have launched a second ship into changing orbits, aimed at solving problems of eventual rendezvous in space.

Monday 13 **"Iron Curtain Drugs"** A deal has been reached between the government and British firms to import drugs from Poland and Italy to supply the NHS. This continues Mr Powell's policy for obtaining cheaper drugs from international sources.

Tuesday 14 **"Budget Day"** The Chancellor of the Exchequer increased indirect taxes to raise £100m. Duty goes up on tobacco, beer, wines, and spirits. This means 1d on a pint on beer, 3d on a bottle of wine and 3s on a bottle on spirits. Cigarettes costing 4s or more for 20 will go up by 4d and cheaper brands by 3d.

HERE IN BRITAIN
"Women Drivers"

Many experts in the motoring industry are calling for more female input in the ergonomic design of new motor vehicles.

'Average female testers' are called for, to ergonomically test new vehicles, as *'pedals which seem fine to the male driver may not be so for a woman wearing spike heels, or a seat back which is fine for a man may not be right for a woman with a tight girdle; seats which may support a man may ruin a nylon dress, or may let a woman wearing one slide excessively, and so on'.*

AROUND THE WORLD
"Fewer Fast Ships for Mail"

Mail being sent to the United States is taking longer to reach its destination, with reports saying that mail didn't arrive until a month after sending. According to the Post Office, there are fewer fast vessels for the Atlantic run than there have been in the past.

Before the last war, a Post Office official said, there were regular sailings from Southampton on four days every week, of liners capable of crossing the Atlantic in four or five days. Now there are far fewer, and they can take up to ten days.

Unsung Heroes Of The Sea

Last year, without publicity and fanfare, Lifeboatmen saved the lives of 354 people, according to their recently published yearly report. Perhaps because lifeboatmen are characteristically unostentatious about their work, perhaps because the service they perform makes no financial demands on the ratepayer or taxpayer, many people seem unaware of the hundreds of lives they save each year and the risks and discomfort they undergo. The lifeboat is expected to be at hand when needed, like the police car, the fire engine or the ambulance. That the Royal National Life-boat Institution is supported entirely by voluntary subscriptions probably only occurs to the average person for a few moments a year when he sees a collection box or a poster appealing for funds.

Yet in coastal towns and villages the threat of disaster at sea is more imminent, the lifeboat service is more familiar and volunteers to man the boats continue to come forward and the service is steadily modernising and improving its efficiency with new boats and liaison with other rescue services. A less tangible development in recent years has been the change in the nature of the services the lifeboatmen have been called on to perform. The decline of the fishing industry in many parts of the country has been accompanied by a phenomenal increase in the number of pleasure-boat owners, causing even more work for the Institution.

As an official put it, the institution's charter is to rescue people from the sea without distinction between nationalities or circumstances and this includes 'bloody fools' as much as those who are victims of an Act of God. A glance at the accounts of rescues in the institution's quarterly journal will convince both the unfortunate and the foolish how great is their debt to those who uncomplainingly risk their lives time and again to save others.

April 15th – 21st 1964

IN THE NEWS

Wednesday 15 — **"Bristol Holdup"** 30 ships are waiting to be unloaded at Bristol docks where over 2,000 men are idle having joined their colleagues at Avonmouth on strike.

Thursday 16 — **"Colour TV"** Although no system has yet been adopted, Britain should have a full colour TV service no later than 1967. The final decision on the format will be made in April 1965.

Friday 17 — **"Inside the Beating Heart"** For the first time ever, scientists in Chicago have seen inside a living heart. They inserted a thin tube holding a microscopic camera, into a living dog, without having to cut open its chest.

Saturday 18 — **"The Great Escape"** Two German youths have escaped to the west in a light aircraft. Neither of them had any prior piloting experience, but they were undetected by East German police, and landed in a cornfield near Minden.

Sunday 19 — **"Welsh Nuclear Power"** The National Grid is set to receive Welsh nuclear power later this year. Trawsfynydd is the fifth power station of its type to produce nuclear power for British electricity.

Monday 20 — **"Black Out Wrecks BBC 2's First Night"** A power breakdown plunged the television centre at Shepherd's Bush into darkness and chaos a few minutes before the new BBC2 channel was due to air for the first time. All programmes were cancelled.

Tuesday 21 — **"Parachute Drop Gone Wrong"** Over 11,000 lbs worth of dummy ammunition landed on a train track in Cambridge just minutes before a train was due. The load was part of an army supply drop, and the RAF have commissioned an investigation into what might have resulted in a fatal accident.

HERE IN BRITAIN

"The Little Perishers"

Lord Kilbrandon is amongst many who think that the current Juvenile Court system is too informal and that it is not setting children up for the severity of the law as an adult.

Instead, people like Kilbrandon are more in favour of *'frightening the living daylights out of them'* by using the more formal channels. His view is there is much to be said for delivering the juvenile *'little perisher'* to an *'ugly, uniformed, Superintendent'* at an *'ugly police station'* rather than the *'mollycoddling and reassuring environment of the juvenile court'*.

AROUND THE WORLD

"The Perisher Valley"

Work is in the closing stages for the building of the highest church in Australia, in the rapidly expanding Perisher Valley, New South Wales. The team is working tirelessly to complete the construction before the onslaught of the Australian winter, which would prohibit them from working for the next few months.

The Perisher Valley has undergone an impressive level of growth in recent years, going from a remote settlement with only nine small lodges just five years ago, to a bustling ski resort today, with two hotels, 50 private lodges and 13 ski-lifts.

LITTLE OOKPIK

A native interpretation of the Arctic Owl, the Canadian Board of Trade and Commerce is looking for world markets to sell their 'Little Ookpik' 6" high, Eskimo doll, which is to become the official mascot of Canada in future trade exhibitions across the world. The inspiration for the doll came from the Canadian trade exhibition held in Sydney last summer, where officials found an image of a kangaroo reaching into her pouch and drawing out a maple leaf and saying 'Look What I Found'; these images captured the minds of the Australian people helping to make the Sydney exhibition such a success. The Ookpik acts as the perfect mascot for Canada, wide-eyed, quirky and mysterious, creating not only a poignant cultural point, but also an exciting and somewhat random toy.

A new mascot was required for the scheduled Canadian Fair in Philadelphia in November and was of the utmost importance as the British have a similar fair a month before Canada, meaning competition is high. Advertisements showcasing the doll as inextricably linked with the Canadian Fair with the slogan 'Ookpik is Coming' have been circulated round both Canada and the United States, to such an extent that a Philadelphian television producer refused to do a programme about the fair without the presence of one of the toys, a toy which the Ottawa Council couldn't locate. Delays have been encountered on the toys' production line due to a recent run on seal skins.

After finally 'cobbling together' a toy, with the help of a Royal Canadian Navy surgeon who sewed on new feet, it was put 'pride of place' at the Northern Affairs display at the fair, where cash orders exceeded 12,000. There is more demand for the Ookpik toy than there are toys available, with a steadily growing backlog of orders.

APRIL 22ᴿᴰ - 28ᵀᴴ 1964

IN THE NEWS

Wednesday 22   "**Berlin Exchange**" Greville Wynne was returned from a Russian gaol back to his family as he was exchanged for Western prisoner Gordon Lonsdale at a Berlin checkpoint. Wynne had been sentenced in Moscow to eight years 'deprivation of liberty' for espionage.

Thursday 23   "**Is it Gold?**" There was a major security presence at London Airport when a Russian TU-104 airliner touched down from Moscow carrying a cargo described as 'nine tons of metal', believed to be gold worth nearly £4m.

Friday 24   "**Neither Drunk nor Disorderly**" Recent figures show that there has been a substantial decrease in drunkenness amongst young people in recent years. This is supported by lower crime rates, especially in Central London and the Midlands.

Saturday 25   "**Mermaid Head Missing**" The Danish police were hard at work throughout the day in a desperate search for the sawn-off head of the 'Little Mermaid', a statue that had stood pride of place in the Copenhagen Harbour for over 50 years.

Sunday 26   "**Pin Money Carpetbaggers**" This is just one of the unfavourable nicknames given to 'amateurs' in the television and film industry by their professional counterparts at the British Actors' Equity Association in London, as they petition for tougher acting credential requirements.

Monday 27   "**Choice of Pirates**" A new pirate radio station has dropped anchor just off the Essex Naze, and far enough out to escape the jurisdiction of Mr Bevins and the British authorities. The station is to be called Radio Atlanta.

Tuesday 28   "**Close Early Campaign**" After attacks on proprietors, a coffee shop in Colchester has begun a 'close early campaign' to teach rowdy teenagers a lesson.

HERE IN BRITAIN

"Shakespeare's Birthday"

Ambassadors from many different countries flocked to Stratford Upon Avon, the birthplace of famous playwright William Shakespeare. The Queen, in an address read for her by Lord Avon to a number of important people including the Duke of Edinburgh, actors and actresses from the stage, and 750 members of the Diplomatic Corps, spoke highly of Shakespeare, talking about how *'The treasure of his legacy to our nation and to the world at large is beyond estimation … he had in abundance the two great gifts of humanity-the gifts of laughter and compassion'.*

AROUND THE WORLD

"La Pieta"

For the first time ever, the famous Michelangelo statue 'La Pieta', has made a journey out of the Vatican City. She has gone to New York for the World's Fair, having first received a blessing from the Pope. However, critics and the public alike have criticised the poor display of the statue at the fair. Hardly doing justice to the magnificent piece, not only is the statue concealed behind a bulletproof plastic curtain, but it is lit up by a bright blue light, obscuring vision and taking away from the brilliant white marble.

NEW YORK WORLD FAIR

President Johnson officially opened the New York World's Fair, with spirits not dampened by the persisting onslaught of rain nor the civil rights protestors, who largely unsuccessfully, attempted to disrupt proceedings by forming roadblocks and staging protests throughout the city. The 'biggest fair ever staged' as it's been called by the event organisers, is expected to receive over 500,000 visitors on the first day alone, and 200 pavilions are set up and ready to greet them.

The title of crème de la crème of exhibits, however, is won by General Motors, who paid over $50 million, the value of roughly 7,000 Cadillacs, for their stand. The vice president of the company has justified the excessive spend on the demonstration by saying that the money was spent *'to get people in a good mood, to get them thinking big',* and in turn one can only assume he hopes that because of it, people will buy more Cadillacs.

The New York World's Fair was held between October and April in both 1964 and 1965 and was a showcase of 20th Century American business and culture. At a time where public consumerism was a policy being encouraged by the US government, the Western world were invited in to see the products of the 'American Dream' and the triumphant success of the Capitalist system. In that sense, the Fair was an opportunity to explore modern advancements in technology, eat and drink traditional American food and bathe in the successes of small American businesses, but for America itself it was far bigger than that. The country invited not only the Western World, but the Soviet Union and its satellite states, thus turning 'expo' into a political statement, triumphantly showing off the US' economic boom, and showcasing Capitalist ideology to all major world powers.

April 29th – May 5th 1964

IN THE NEWS

Wednesday 29   **"Swift, Silent and Serene"** Are just three of the adjectives that have been used to describe the new BOAC VC10 as it left London on its first ever scheduled service to Lagos. Sporting a smart new blue and gold livery, the brand-new Vickers VC10 airliner both looks and sounds the part of BOAC's flagship aircraft.

Thursday 30   **"Strength in Numbers"** Over 3 million engineers have threatened an overtime ban if the 40-hour week is not agreed to by September. The committee of the Engineering Union has sanctioned the severe actions in an attempt to get government approval.

Friday 1 May   **"Princess Margaret's Baby"** The Royal household has confirmed that Princess Margaret has given birth to a daughter at Kensington Palace, and that both mother and daughter are healthy and in good spirits.

Saturday 2   **"Victory at Last"** For the first time in their history, West Ham United have won the FA Cup, beating Preston North End 3-2 at Wembley Stadium.

Sunday 3   **"Just 'Popping' In"** Billy J Kramer and the band The Dakotas were forced to flee an onslaught of charging fans who stormed the barriers to the private home of the Marquess of Bath, where the band was performing a private concert.

Monday 4   **"Time To Go"** The Times Newspaper office in Moscow has been forced to close, and its Russian correspondent has been expelled from the country, following the Soviet government's belief that the newspaper was *'intentionally slandering the Soviet Union'*.

Tuesday 5   **"Aden Offensive"** 3,000 British troops have gathered to take operational control of the Dhala road that runs between Yemen and Aden. Guerrilla attacks have plagued the route for months.

HERE IN BRITAIN

"Victorious Welcome"

West Ham's triumphant return to East London after their FA Cup final victory over Preston North End drew out crowds of over 250,000, and balloons, streamers and coloured pictures of the cup winners lined the streets.

The official welcome by the East Ham Mayor was cancelled, with a turnout of over 7,000 people gathered outside the town hall making a proper reception impossible. Police leave was suspended, and one officer, who has served for over 30 years said, *'I have never seen a procession in East London like it. It is like the coronation.'*

AROUND THE WORLD

"A Bantam's Duty"

Two Bantam hens have been assigned to the US wildlife research station in Lafayette, Louisiana, to sit on a pair of crane eggs until they hatch. The hens were specially selected due to their impressive sitting capacity, and yet the task may prove a struggle for even them, as the eggs are almost as big as they are.

Once hatched, the cranes can grow as tall as 5 feet, dwarfing the bantam hens. The US government, although not hopeful the experiment will be successful, is nonetheless committed to increasing the crane population in America.

Antarctic Struggles

Signy Island (bottom) and the RRS John Briscoe (above).

For the first time in 21 years, Britain will no longer have an ongoing Antarctic operation following the close of the season. There are currently six permanent stations, manned by 105 men, which are to be shut down for the time being after three very successful years of Antarctic exploration. The last season, however, has proved to be far more troublesome, as relieving the stations has proved to be no mean feat.

The first issue came when the RRS Shackleton was attempting to deliver material for a large new biological factory on Signy Island, one of the British Antarctic outposts thousands of miles from civilisation. On a route that was normally trouble free for larger ships, the RRS Shackleton was trapped by over 40 miles of thick ice, delaying its arrival by over 3 weeks. Forced to divert, the Shackleton, along with the RRS John Briscoe instead attempted to reach Deception Island, 500 miles west of Signy. This too was fraught with troubles, as they were once again trapped by thick ice. Trouble with the reconnaissance aircraft left the possibility of the ships being stuck in the open all winter if it wasn't for the ingenuity of members of the Survey, who successfully transported spares between the ship and the airstrip across 30 miles of sea ice and the cliffs of Adelaide Island.

The RRS Shackleton is commissioned for a further five years of exploration and has recently endured a severe storm that forced the breakup of a 12-mile-long iceberg in the ship's waters. The skill of the captain, and a large degree of luck, was all that saved the Royal Research Ship from sinking. Nevertheless, there are detailed and developed plans for the future of British Antarctic exploration, including marine diving work, geological lake studies, and ice examinations.

May 6th - 12th 1964
IN THE NEWS

Wednesday 6 — **"North Sea Oil"** The Minister of Power is to allow the issue of licenses to oil companies wishing to explore for natural gas and oil in the British controlled North Sea. 20 applicants are expected, only three of whom are British.

Thursday 7 — **"The Kennedy Appeal"** An appeal has officially been made for donations to the 'Kennedy Appeal' to fund the education of selected British students at the Massachusetts Institute of Technology in America.

Friday 8 — **"Labour Triumph"** Labour made a gain of 250 seats in the local council elections, delivering a sweeping blow to Sir Alec Douglas Home's Conservative Government.

Saturday 9 — **"Revolver Mystery"** The owner of the gun that shot the pilot of a twin-engine airliner that crashed in California with the loss of 44 lives, has been revealed as the same passenger who had taken out a life insurance policy worth over $60,000 last month.

Sunday 10 — **"1-2 on the Streets of Monaco"** In a double team victory, BRM's 1962 Formula One World Champion Graham Hill came home to win the Monaco Grand Prix, with his teammate, American, R. Ginther, in second place.

Monday 11 — **"Biggest Tanker on the Mersey"** Watched by crowds of spectators, the largest ship ever to enter the Mersey, the tanker Berge Bergeson (870ft long), successfully negotiated the notorious Dog Leg in the channel and berthed at the Tranmere oil terminal.

Tuesday 12 — **"The Big Spring-clean"** The cleaning of St. Paul's Cathedral began with the first stage, the lower sections, to take up to 18 months and cost £70,000. The whole job is to be done entirely with water and 'elbow grease'

HERE IN BRITAIN

"Hair Tint Fear"

Women are refraining from hair tints due to a fear over what their husbands might say, a recent report suggests. The British woman *'lags behind her European counterpart'* and is *'far behind her American sister'* when it comes to hair cosmetics and accessories, despite the recent developments in hair cosmetic technology.

The Master of the Incorporated Guild of Hairdressers, Wigmakers and Perfumers has suggested that the reluctance must come from women being 'under a man's thumb', as he can see no other reason why women would not want to embrace an artist's *'rainbow palette'*.

AROUND THE WORLD

"Instant Igloo"

The Ontario research foundation has developed what has become known as an 'instant igloo', designed to be a great aid to both civilians and military personnel working in very cold climates. The ingenious design is made from a foamy plastic material which becomes a semi-rigid structure once a match is put to it.

The igloo works via an inbuilt heat source which, when set on fire, causes a rapid expansion of the foam into a 3" thick wall. The plan is to make the shelter an essential for the tool kits of all cold weather operators.

Zoo Doctors

There is a reason why it takes longer to become a vet than it does a doctor, and of course, once realised, it seems glaringly obvious and makes total sense. The main difference, naturally, is that animals can't talk back to tell you what is wrong with them, a fact that, if different, would significantly help the job of the zoologist society and zoo doctors, who held their annual general meeting earlier this week.

Zoo doctors, as explained by an enthusiastic young veterinary officer, are forced to not only console and look after many different species of, often dangerous, exotic, animals, but also diagnose and treat them in the best way possible. A zoo doctor might see a meerkat, penguin and lion across their table in the same day and be expected to have the skills necessary to deal with all of them. It can safely be assumed that being a zoo doctor needs a great degree of professional ingenuity, and as the Zoological society launched their new Institute of Comparative Physiology, they showcased many of the animals that had received treatment by members of the institution and boasting the *'best zoo doctors in the world'*. Certainly, the numbers seem to back this claim up, with recovery rates of large animals increasing from 40% to 80% across 3,000 cases in the last 10 years.

Not only are doctors responsible for nursing ill creatures back to health, but their role also extends to species preservation, and they are often tasked with the collection of semen in rare animals, and blood tests for experiments and research purposes. The most recent of these tests was to determine whether North American and European Bison were genetically identical; for those interested in the etymological differences between intercontinental bison, it turns out they differ significantly.

May 13th – 19th 1964

IN THE NEWS

Wednesday 13 — **"Jaguar Strike"** Over 5,000 men from Jaguar Daimler have been ordered to return to work by the Engineering Union, after 2,500 more Jaguar employees, joined the 3,000 on strike from Daimler.

Thursday 14 — **"Revolutionary Hospital"** The Minister of Health has announced plans to replace the run-down St Alfege's Hospital in Greenwich with a new, state of the art, prefabricated one. The new hospital will have 800 beds and cost between £5.5 and £6 million.

Friday 15 — **"New Scotland Yard"** Scotland Yard is to be relocated to a site on Victoria Street, Broadway, that not only gives the agency more space, but also a more modern and sufficient headquarters.

Saturday 16 — **"Ford Support for ITA"** The American Ford Foundation has committed to donating over £100,000 to help British research into their Initial Teaching Alphabet scheme to help young people learn how to read in a more efficient and effective way.

Sunday 17 — **"Mods Vs Rockers"** Fights at three coastal resorts broke out between youths involving over 2,000 people. In Brighton, a promenade skirmish caused five girls to be taken to hospital, and at Bournemouth over 40 people were arrested in a local gang fight.

Monday 18 — **"Guilty but Insane"** The House of Lords has deemed the courts verdict of 'guilty but insane' to be equal to an acquittal and have suggested a 'not guilty by reason of insanity' would make more sense. The old verdict dates to the Trial of Lunatics in 1883.

Tuesday 19 — **"No Smooth Running"** The Crystal Palace National Recreation Centre has been forced to cancel its first large athletics event because of the 'unsatisfactory nature of the track'.

HERE IN BRITAIN

"The Weather Master"

A South African has become an entrant to the Warwickshire County Cricket Club's £500 competition to find *'an effective wicket cover'* by claiming an ability to control the weather. The entrepreneur has expressed his desire to come to England and show off his weather changing capability, after claiming success in America, Canada and Europe.

British weather will be *'easy to master'* according to the South African, whose company claims to be able to break up clouds above certain areas, eliminating rain, smog and overcast skies. The cricket club has thanked the man for his suggestion.

AROUND THE WORLD

"Supersonic Flights"

The time and effort gone into making the possibility of supersonic flight a reality appears to be only half the challenge when it comes to its implementation in commercial air travel. People living on the flight paths of major US airports have caused so much uproar about the sonic boom trials over Oklahoma, that a court order was issued to suspend them.

Some 2,800 damage claims, 5,000 noise complaints and one complaint by a woman who said that *'the noise and shock waves of the sonic boom were enough to break her brassiere'*, have been reported.

Whit Walks

This week, Whit Sunday was celebrated around the world by Catholics, Anglicans and Methodists. This special day is celebrated to commemorate the descent of the Holy Spirit upon Christ's disciples and is the seventh day after Easter or Pentecost, its name deriving from the Anglo-Saxon word 'wit' meaning 'understanding' to celebrate the disciples being filled with the wisdom of the Holy Spirit.

Whit Monday was officially recognised as a bank holiday in 1871 and the day has a special cultural significance in the north-west of England. Many workplaces including factories and cotton mills closed for the whole Whitsuntide week giving workers a holiday and towns held fairs, markets, and parades. Still, a major tradition is the 'Whit Walk' when local churches or chapels employ bands to lead traditional processions through the streets and this year a 70-year-old housewife took part in her 60th Manchester Whit Walk. The origin of these processions dates back to July 1821 when the children of Manchester commemorated the coronation of George IV and children of all denominations walked in procession from their schools and assembled at Ardwick Green to sing 'God Save the King'.

The Bradford Whit Walk has been held continuously since 1903 and is one of the most popular events on the race-walking calendar, attracting hundreds of entries. At the height of its popularity, it attracted top British race walkers and in the 20s and 30s was recognised as the breeding ground for British Olympians, with winners Tommy Green and Harold Whitlock going on to win Olympic gold medals in 1932 and 1936 respectively. This is also the week for many local brass band contests and workers to take the opportunity to enjoy canal boat rides, go to the races and of course, go to the seaside.

May 20th - 26th 1964

IN THE NEWS

Wednesday 20 — "Microphones in Moscow" United States Ambassadors in Russia have discovered a network of over 40 microphones embedded in the walls of their Moscow Embassy. They have been there since as early as 1953.

Thursday 21 — "Less Beef for Your Pound" Housewives may have to pay up to 14s (70p) per lb for beef as continental demand and a decrease in Argentine landings makes the meat more expensive.

Friday 22 — "Eyesight Requirement" To accommodate the smaller font of the new seven symbol number plate, eyesight requirements to obtain a driving license are changing. Road users now must read the number plate from 67ft. away rather than 75ft.

Saturday 23 — "The Strike of the Sugar Workers" Tensions in British Guinea are reaching new highs as British troops are being sent to restore order after violence broke out between local groups. The 18th week of sugar worker strikes have led to violent terror attacks.

Sunday 24 — "Public Rights Suspended in Peru" At least 300 people have been killed after an unpopular decision by a referee at a soccer match in Lima, led to violence across the country. The government has declared a state of emergency.

Monday 25 — "Lost in Space" The US have lost nearly $1 million worth of radioactive plutonium 238, after human error prevented a navigational satellite, powered by the plutonium, from entering orbit. The toxic metal was immediately vaporised.

Tuesday 26 — "Typhoid from One Tin of Beef" Just one tin of beef has been identified as the cause of a typhoid outbreak in Aberdeen. The contamination is thought to have happened abroad.

HERE IN BRITAIN

"Sound Guide"

The British museum has become one of the first in the world to introduce a portable machine known as the 'Sound Guide' for ongoing audio commentary for visitors to hire. The device, having been tested at the Imperial War Museum, launched with a demonstration of a tour of the Elgin Marbles.

Its simple controls, having only access to a 'go' and 'stop' button, coupled with its ergonomically designed earpieces, are proving to be very popular amongst tourists, and the Windsor Castle Association will implement its own 45-minute version at the Castle from next week.

AROUND THE WORLD

"Bullfighters Recognition to Fleming"

Inscribed with the words 'To Dr Fleming, with the gratitude of bullfighters' a monument has been opened in Madrid commemorating Sir Alexander Fleming and his discovery of the penicillin drug. The memorial encompasses a full bronze statue of Fleming with a Spanish bullfighter stood in front, saluting the scientist with his montera (a matador's hat), and is located not far from the city's famous fighting arena.

The speech by the mayor, with the British ambassador in attendance, thanked Dr Fleming for his services to science, and for inadvertently saving the lives of many bullfighters.

ROLLS MEETS ROYCE

Charles Rolls (left) and Henry Royce (right) with the first ever Rolls Royce car.

To celebrate the 60th anniversary of the now legendary Rolls-Royce car brand, a pageant of Rolls Royce and Bentley cars was held at Goodwood motor circuit this week. Over 1,000 cars attended the rally that ran from 9am. Judges began circulating the paddock at around 11am, when men could still be seen feverishly polishing pristine bodywork, cleaning wheels not out of place on a royal coach and scrubbing engine bays clean enough to eat dinner from. The British culture epitomised by the Rolls-Royce brand is not to be understated, and the cars have become one of Britain's most famous exports, acting as an ambassador of class at every corner of the globe.

Mr Charles Rolls first met Mr Henry Royce at a Manchester hotel in 1904. Rolls, the son of a Lord, was an ex-Etonian and held an engineering degree from Cambridge. By contrast, Royce was the son of a flour miller from Peterborough, whose first job was as a scarecrow on a farm. By this point however, both were relatively successful yet minor businessmen, with Rolls owning a small dealership selling French cars in London, and Royce having just built his first vehicle, the Royce 10hp motor car. The chance meeting of the two men forged a partnership that gifted the world with such elegant machines as the Silver Ghost and the Silver Cloud, not to mention aircraft engines powering the likes of Supermarine Spitfires.

The prizes for the pageant were presented by the Duchess of Richmond, whose husband owns the track and the Goodwood Estate. Ironically, because he did not drive a Bentley or a Rolls-Royce on his return to the Estate, the Duke was refused entry three times to his own racing track by an amateur steward! The volunteer was suitably mortified when he was enlightened.

May 27th – June 2nd 1964

IN THE NEWS

Wednesday 27   **"India Mourns"** News of the death of India's first independent leader, Pandit Jawaharlal Nehru, has reached the furthest corners of India and thousands are in mourning. The new leader will be chosen tomorrow.

Thursday 28   **"Pirate Radio Landing"** The pirate radio station, Radio Sutch, has begun broadcasting from the unmanned Shivering Sands Army Fort in the middle of the Thames Estuary. The station will be visited by Kent police and the War Office in the hope of removing 'the trespassers.'

Friday 29   **"The Bull Ring Centre"** The Duke of Edinburgh has officially opened what has been hailed as the *'most advanced shopping centre in the world'* in central Birmingham. The centre covers 3.8 acres of land and cost around £8 million to build.

Saturday 30   **"Typhoid City Shuts School"** Typhoid cases in Aberdeen have risen to 136. All schools are now closed and a special hospital has been erected just outside the city centre.

Sunday 31   **"Factory Built Housing"** The Government has revealed new plans for a revolutionary factory system to build houses, bringing the usual 12 week build time down to just a week. A high proportion of steel fabrication techniques will be used.

Mon 1 June   **"Little Mermaid Returns"** The Little Mermaid statue, *'the darling of the whole world'*, has taken her place back on the Copenhagen seafront with a replacement head. Her 'previous head' was sawn off last month in an act of vandalism.

Tuesday 2   **"Nuclear Ship"** The world's first nuclear-powered merchant vessel, the Savannah, will sail her maiden transatlantic voyage from New York to Germany, Ireland and Britain, and back to New York in June.

HERE IN BRITAIN
"Cuddlesome Pets"

'Cuddlesome Pets' is the name given to the popular band The Beatles by psychologist Dr Casson, writing in the 'Family Doctor'. His theory is that very young girls are attracted to the music of the band due to their 'classless' nature and modest dress, coupled with their mophead hair. Young children, uncorrupted by the world, appear to be drawn to the stars, whose fame has not manifested itself in flashy clothes and theatrical stage presence. He puts 'Beatlemania' in adolescents down to *'an inability to refrain from 'letting go' when surrounded by hysterical behaviour.'*

AROUND THE WORLD
"Weeping Thousands"

Over 250,000 grief-stricken people made the trip to visit the body of Indian Prime Minister Jawaharlal Nehru placed on the porch of his house in New Deli. The death of the 74-year-old was not unexpected, but nonetheless shocked the nation, and thousands of mourners witnessed Mr Nehru's cremation on the banks of the Jumna River near the spot where Mahatma Gandhi was cremated some 16 years ago. Mr Nehru was beloved and honoured with the name 'Panditji' to the thousands he led since Indian independence in 1947. The Indian leader died without naming a successor.

Drapers Company

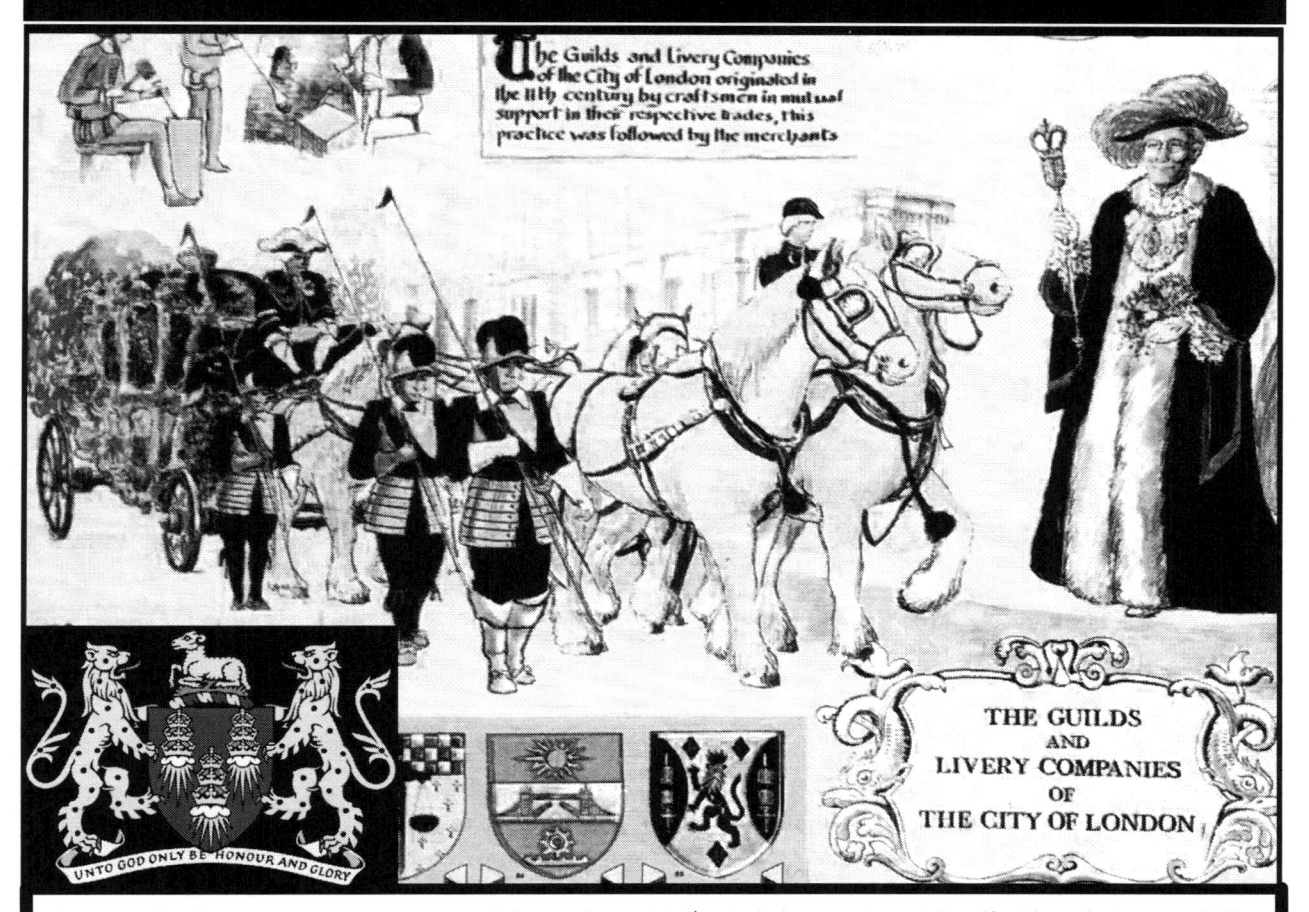

This week, the Drapers Company celebrated its 600th Birthday at St Michael's Church in Cornhill, Central London. Not only is the company steeped with history and tradition, its maintenance of standards and adaptation to the largest degree of change seen in human history over the last 200 years, is an element that should be respected and admired. The company was formed as a militant organisation designed to protect and monopolise the industry of drapery. The company was officially awarded monopoly of the drapery trade in 1364, but the company ran into issues in the early 1500s, when the monopoly became impossible to enforce, and the company was forced to hire many non-drapers as it strayed away from its namesake business. Their books prove that many of the wealthy businessmen involved with the trade cared more about land and money than the industry itself.

The title of a 'Livery company', dates back to as early as the first guilds in the 12th Century. As society developed, and the earliest forms of British capitalism grew in fruition, these guilds became more individualised, often characterising themselves by specific clothes, or 'liveries', to distinguish themselves from other guilds. By the 14th Century, there were 48 well-established companies that had earned political influence with the Lord Mayor through charters and ordinances. Now, livery companies are one of the cornerstones for political operation in London, responsible for the election of Sheriffs of the City of London and hold large influence with the mayor. Many livery companies still support various alms-houses across the country and sit on a dedicated committee, helping to seek joint initiatives for the future; in essence, the livery companies control much of London both politically and financially, and often work together across multiple industries to foster support for their own interests.

June 3rd - 9th 1964

IN THE NEWS

Wednesday 3 — **"Hovercraft Trial"** An SRN3 hovercraft has been handed over to the Ministry of Defence to undergo trials on its effectiveness as a military vehicle. It will undergo tests in coastal defence, landings and anti-submarine roles.

Thursday 4 — **"Clean Up TV"** Supporters of the clean-up television campaign have been asked by the League of Women to switch off their TV's between 9pm and 10pm on June 14th to demonstrate to the BBC and ITA the effect on ratings should they boycott specific programmes in the future.

Friday 5 — **"Blue Streak Failure"** In Australia, Britain's Blue Streak rocket broke up - as scheduled, mid-flight, just nine minutes after its successful launch. The rocket reached speeds of over 8,500mph and an altitude of 150 miles.

Saturday 6 — **"Churchill College"** The Duke of Edinburgh paid tribute to the wartime Prime Minister at the opening of the Churchill College at Cambridge University. Lady Churchill and a number of Sir Winston's relatives were present at the ceremony.

Sunday 7 — **"Better Teeth for Birmingham"** Birmingham City Council has become the first in Britain to add fluoride to its water as an official policy, not just an experiment.

Monday 8 — **"Ashes to the Ganges"** The ashes of former Indian Prime Minister Mr Nehru, were today released with full religious and military honours, into India's holiest body of water at the confluence of the Ganges and Jumna rivers.

Tuesday 9 — **"Doors Closed"** Britain is no longer accepting applications from unskilled workers from Pakistan and India who are wishing to come and work in Great Britain. Last year alone, Britain received over 60,000 people, 40,000 of whom were from India and Pakistan.

HERE IN BRITAIN

"Picture Collection Destroyed"

A collection of over one million postcards, containing photos of almost every town in the south and west of England and south Wales, are to be destroyed. Miss Winifred Ridley held the postcards, the photographs taken between 1900 and 1940 by her father, a professional photographer, together with thousands of glass negatives, in a workshop behind her house in Bournemouth, but now she must move out to make way for a new development and has nowhere to store her immense collection. Miss Ridley, who once earned 2s a week colouring the views, is *'heartbroken'*.

AROUND THE WORLD

"Sterilising Starlings"

The latest development in the Unites States' war against starlings is a new chemical designed to sterilise the birds during their mating season. There are estimated to be over 500 million in the US, causing in excess of $50 million worth of damage every year to crops.

The birds are not native to America, and were brought over by an avid Shakespeare fan, who wanted the US to experience the birds spoken about in the playwrights' work. In Washington, 100 public buildings are wired to give starlings an electric shock when they alight on any ledges.

D-Day Anniversary

The Normandy beaches have been invaded once again, this time by thousands of British, American, Canadian, and French troops, who gathered to commemorate the 20th anniversary of the D-Day landings. General Charles De Gaulle was conspicuously and unsurprisingly absent, and General Eisenhower and Field Marshall Lord Montgomery, were both unable to make the trip, but the British and American delegations were nonetheless unusually strong in D-Day commanders.

In 1944, throughout the build-up to D-Day, General Eisenhower used several tactics and strategies to purposefully mislead the Nazi commanders into thinking the offensive was going to be staged at the Pas de Calais, rather than the Normandy beaches. Calais was the logical choice for such an attack, being the French point closest to mainland England, thus the deception did not require much convincing. Not only did Eisenhower 'leak' fake information through double agents, including a wild suggestion of Norway being a key landing spot, but also organised practical deceptions.

A 'ghost army', under the command of George Patton, was sent to Calais together with a fake Mulberry Harbour, in such a way that it diverted attention away from the Normandy beaches, and many fraudulent radio-transmissions were planted. On the day, mine sweepers began to clear channels for the invasion fleet under cover of the bombing which began at midnight and finished just after dawn without encountering the enemy. Despite extensive planning and deception, the D-Day operation began far from smoothly. The day selected for the invasion, the 5th of July, was plagued with exceptionally rough seas, thus it was delayed by a further 24 hours, which increased the risk of German awareness. Nevertheless, the deception element of Operation Overlord proved to be an astounding success, with the Germans being unprepared for an invasion in Normandy.

June 10th - 16th 1964

IN THE NEWS

Wednesday 10 — **"US Army Minis"** The United States army are testing left hand drive variations of British Motor Corporation Minis to assess how suitable the vehicles would be for the service.

Thursday 11 — **"Free Nelson Mandela"** Nelson Mandela is among seven men who have been arrested and sentenced to life in prison by the South African Government. They were found guilty of planning a 'violent' revolution against the country's racial policies.

Friday 12 — **"Breaking Point"** The Liverpool Docks have been brought almost to a standstill as over 8,000 men left their posts and went on strike. The unofficial strike came as a result of rumoured pay cuts, with bonuses supposedly to be cut in half.

Saturday 13 — **"Queen's Birthday Honours"** To celebrate her official birthday, Her Majesty appointed many citizens of the Commonwealth realms to various orders and honours. They are both reward and recognition of their good works.

Sunday 14 — **"World Weather Watch"** The World Meteorological Association, after trialling the replacement of manned meteorological stations by automated and semi-automated systems at many locations, plans to roll out the equipment world-wide.

Monday 15 — **"News from Space"** The new $300,000 telescope 'Cassiopeia' has received radio emissions from space for the first time. It is thought that the signals were *'a mere few tens of thousands of light years away'*.

Tuesday 16 — **"Concorde Sell Out"** The prospect of supersonic flight has gripped the nation to such an extent that all the seats on the scheduled flights of Concorde are fully booked already. The aircraft has a topographical navigation display showing passengers a continuous plot of the aircraft's current position

HERE IN BRITAIN

"M1 Racetrack"

The Ministry of Transport is investigating British car manufacturers, who are claimed to have been testing prototype cars along the M1 Motorway. Top speed, durability and economy are all features which can be tested on the motorway, but many are said to have been testing cars built for the Le Mans 24-hour race, approaching speeds of almost 200mph.

A spokesperson for Sunbeam said that whilst there may have been some 'running in', there was *'certainly nothing of a high-speed nature'*. The Minister is to be asked to impose a limit of 100 mph on motorways.

AROUND THE WORLD

"Picture phone"

An invention by The Bell Telephone Company in the United States allows both parties on either end of the phone to see who they are talking to. The initial service will operate from a public booth in New York, Washington, and Chicago.

In New York, the caller will sit approximately three feet from a camera, holding the receiver and will be able to decide if he wants his own picture transmitted or not. He cannot interfere with the picture of the person at the other end. The picture phone will cost the caller $16 for a 3-minute call.

The Queen's Coronation BIRTHDAY PARADE

★ TROOPING THE COLOUR CEREMONY ★

Trooping the Colour proceeded this year with its usual pomp and circumstance when it was the turn of the 1st Battalion, the Coldstream Guards, to perform the ancient ceremony. There was the usual unrehearsed horse falling out of line, which prompted the retort of a woman, clearly from the Midlands of *'what he needs is a kick in the guts and a ploughed field',* much to the amusement of those standing around her. Nevertheless, a stress-free ceremony is a happy ceremony as far as the event organisers are concerned, and the event this year was certainly a ceremonial success with an exceptionally large turnout causing minimal fuss, except for the acres of land left covered in a sea of litter.

Trooping the Colour is a ceremonial military parade that involves the seven army regiments who serve the Queen, grouped under the umbrella of 'The Household Division' come together to celebrate the monarch's birthday. The ceremony is said to have its origins from an ancient Roman military practice in which the regimental standard was marched in front of soldiers who would then be able to identify it on the battlefield. A regiment's colours embody its spirit and service to the home it represents, as well as its fallen soldiers; before and after each battle, the colour party would 'troop' or march their colours through the ranks so that every soldier could see that the colours were intact.

On the battlefield, the flags were used as rallying points and the loss of a colour, or the capture of an enemy colour, were respectively considered the greatest shame, or the greatest glory on a battlefield. For more than 250 years, Trooping the Colour has commemorated the birthday of the sovereign as well as showcasing a display of army drills, music and horsemanship.

JUNE 17TH - 23RD 1964

IN THE NEWS

Wednesday 17 — **"Japan Trade Fair"** The first purpose-built floating trade fair has docked at Tilbury. The Sakura Maru will remain for four days showcasing 22,000 samples of Japanese goods. 18,000 businessmen and women along with a further 10,000 members of the public are expected to attend.

Thursday 18 — **"Ascot Rained Off"** Gold Cup Day at Ascot, the most important meeting of the year, was called off because of a relentless downpour of rain. Lords Cricket Ground also suffered, not a single ball was bowled.

Friday 19 — **"Atlantic Race Record"** Frenchman Eric Tabarly, of the French navy, has won The Observer Trophy and beaten the record for the quickest solo transatlantic crossing in his 45' ketch, Pen-Duick, in a time of 27 days, one hour and 57 minutes.

Saturday 20 — **"Air Strike"** Britain's independent airline pilots are threatening to strike over pay later this month, causing problems for thousands of holidaymakers in the coming weeks. The threat comes just days after a similar pledge by Air Traffic Controllers.

Sunday 21 — **"Ferrari Win at Le Mans"** Ferrari have made a clean sweep once again, finishing in first, second and third as they cruised to victory for the fifth consecutive year. The British entered Ferrari, driven by F1 World Champion Graham Hill, came home in second place.

Monday 22 — **"More Needle Time"** Record playing or 'Needle time', as it is referred to by the BBC, is to be increased across all BBC radio stations to 47 hours a week as a result of an agreement between the Musician's Union and the broadcasting company.

Tuesday 23 — **"Gassy Exploration"** A new natural gas source has been discovered by The German American North Sea Consortium. They stumbled on the source by accident, sending high pressured water some 150 feet in the air.

HERE IN BRITAIN
"The Disease of Disuse"

An eccentric physician has given his views on the 'obesity epidemic' warned of by so many doctors, in a speech to executives. Dr William Evans suggested they should not be worrying unduly about their weight and spoke of wanting a *'lean horse for a long race ... but preferably a Suffolk Punch between the shafts to draw a heavy load'*. However, Dr Evans advised against the *'disease of disuse'*, saying, 'Sell your car; acquire a dog; dismiss the gardener, do it yourself; take up horse-riding; turn to golf and dispense with the caddie.'

AROUND THE WORLD
"Dormitory Classrooms"

'Hypnopedia tuition', the relaying of information to pupils whilst they're sleeping is the strategy of Russian language teachers during a 22 day, or rather night, course. For three weeks, recorded lessons are repeated to normally sleeping pupils at moments of deepest sleep, and they are assessed on their ability to relay the information the following day. As the information is only played for a few tens of minutes at a time, deep sleep is not affected. The preliminary results of the tests are extremely positive.

Summer Solstice

There is ongoing maintenance of the stones around Stonehenge and only Druids will be allowed into the enclosure at the ancient site at the summer solstice this year. Usually, Druids, along with a select few members of the public who get there early enough, are allowed through to the enclosure, but this year the government have deemed there to be too much of a risk to allow the general public.

The solstice is a biannual event that occurs once in the summer and once in the winter when the sun reaches its highest point in the sky from either the North or South Pole. The event is especially important in the calendars of the Druids, whose origins date back to early Celtic culture. Druids were often high-ranking priests and healers who held a special place in the Celtic society and in Irish folklore, druids are often described as serving kings and lords as counsellors and are often blessed with magical powers such as being able to see the future or control the weather. The modern Druid movement is more diverse, concentrating on appreciating and 'syncing' with the natural world but the movement was born out of a respect for the ancient beliefs.

Stonehenge, a prime spot for hippy congregation, is a magnet for the Druid movement during the solstice, maybe because of its unique alignment with the movements of the sun and moon which would have given the ancient Druids a special vantage point from which to observe and chart the movements of the celestial bodies, helping them to better understand the natural rhythms of the world around them and a place of healing and rejuvenation. Today's Druids still hold Stonehenge in high regard, a site with a special place in their hearts and minds.

June 24th – June 30th 1964

IN THE NEWS

Wednesday 24 — **"More Power"** *'There is nothing larger than this moment'* The General Central Electricity Generating Board has been given the green light by the Ministry of Power to go ahead with their new 2 million Kw coal power station at Didcot.

Thursday 25 — **"Total Eclipse of the Moon"** Even with a blanket of cloud, the moon eclipse was clearly visible in the early hours of the morning throughout most of Britain.

Friday 26 — **"Warships Collide"** During the Navy's annual sea-days display in the English Channel, the frigate HMS Salisbury collided with the destroyer HMS Diamond. No one was hurt and both ships safely returned to Portsmouth for repairs.

Saturday 27 — **"Good Character Cards"** The French Secretary of State for Youth and Sport will implement 'good character cards' which assure the good character of hitch hikers.

Sunday 28 — **"Need More Men"** If the shortage of schoolteachers is to be overcome in the next 20 years, the proportion of men in schools must go up. Delegates to the Association of Education Committees conference heard that the profession was *'top heavy with women'*.

Monday 29 — **"Royal Herbarium Library"** The Queen has opened a new herbarium and library at the Royal Botanic Garden in Edinburgh. It contains the most botanical literature outside of London and holds among 12 of the world's best plant specimen collections.

Tuesday 30 — **"ATC to Park Plans"** Air Traffic Control assistants from London Airport have called off their threat to strike after an agreement to hold talks was reached with the Ministry of Aviation. This will avoid holiday disruption for families later this month.

HERE IN BRITAIN

"Bandstand Music Dispute"

The people of Dartmouth are at odds over the playing of music at the bandstand in the centre of town. Recently, music was stopped after numerous complaints from irritable neighbours who claimed that *'they can't hear themselves think'* during the recitals led by volunteers.

Mr Whitemore, who organises 'twist music' sessions for young people, has cancelled his events, claiming that *'the people who complain are making Dartmouth a dead town'*. There were only two hours of music played last week, and *'even that was too much for the grouchy members of the community'*.

AROUND THE WORLD

"As Slow as a Tortoise"

In a strange protest, trade union workers flooded the Plaza de Mayo in Buenos Aires, where the government house is located, with tortoises, which explained the recent days sharp increase in purchases of the animal.

The creatures were all inscribed with slogans across their shells showing phrases such as *'We are the government'* and *'the government on the march.'* President Illlia has often been presented by cartoonists as a tortoise because of his slow handling of pressing issues. As police cleared away the animals, people congregated at the side of the Plaza and cheered.

A New Effigy For Coins

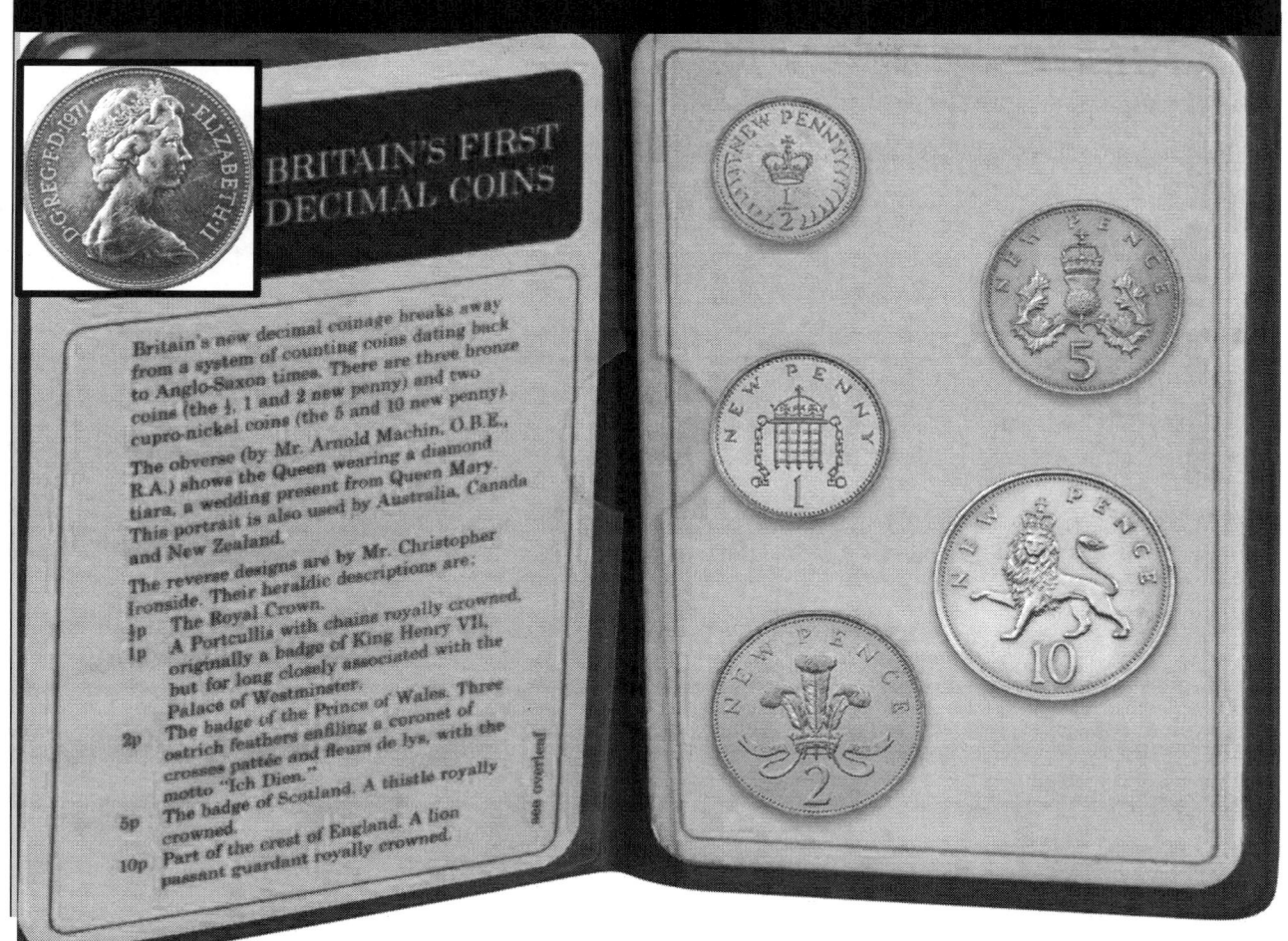

BRITAIN'S FIRST DECIMAL COINS

Britain's new decimal coinage breaks away from a system of counting coins dating back to Anglo-Saxon times. There are three bronze coins (the ½, 1 and 2 new penny) and two cupro-nickel coins (the 5 and 10 new penny).

The obverse (by Mr. Arnold Machin, O.B.E., R.A.) shows the Queen wearing a diamond tiara, a wedding present from Queen Mary. This portrait is also used by Australia, Canada and New Zealand.

The reverse designs are by Mr. Christopher Ironside. Their heraldic descriptions are:

- ½p The Royal Crown.
- 1p A Portcullis with chains royally crowned, originally a badge of King Henry VII, but for long closely associated with the Palace of Westminster.
- 2p The badge of the Prince of Wales. Three ostrich feathers enfiling a coronet of crosses pattée and fleurs de lys, with the motto "Ich Dien."
- 5p The badge of Scotland. A thistle royally crowned.
- 10p Part of the crest of England. A lion passant guardant royally crowned.

Her Majesty the Queen has approved a new effigy for use on coins across the United Kingdom and the Commonwealth. The Queen is depicted simply, facing to the right in accordance with tradition, wearing a plain cloak down at the shoulders and no jewellery other than the diamond tiara given to her as a wedding present by Queen Mary. The effigy will not be implemented immediately on British coins pending a decision on the possible new decimal currency (Editor Note: which was in 1971).

There have been no changes to the effigy on the United Kingdom coins since the reign of Queen Victoria, apart from those necessitated by a change in monarch, with the exception of the head of George V, which was reduced in size slightly to *'prevent ghosting'*. Other minor modifications to beard length and hairstyle were also carried out on His Majesty's coins, but this was more to do with developments in coin stamping machinery rather than a need to change the image.

During the reign of Queen Victoria, the famous and immensely popular 'bun' penny, introduced in 1860 depicts the Queen shown as a graceful young girl with her hair tied back in a neat bun, even though the Queen was at this point over 40. The last coin of the late Queen Victoria was a profound disappointment to everybody and no coin in modern times has aroused such scorn and ridicule. *'Victoria was shown as a rather beaky, austere, and elderly woman, smothered in jewellery and orders, wearing a skimpy veil and an absurd little crown that seemed in danger of toppling from her head'.* The issue had a short life and was replaced in 1893 by a new effigy - a harmless design showing the Queen as a benign and soberly dressed monarch.

JULY 1ST - 7TH 1964

IN THE NEWS

Wednesday 1 — **"TV Station Beats Strike"** Office boys, secretaries, odd-job men, clerks, executives, and directors worked together to give viewers in the border towns of England and southern Scotland a television service for the evening. Border Television, which operates from Carlisle, beat a strike by screening a programme of news, features and films.

Thursday 2 — **"Unilever to Farm Fish"** British company Unilever is to start salmon and trout mass production. Experts are currently looking for a suitable fish farm location, likely to be in one of the Scottish lochs.

Friday 3 — **"Pirate Radio Legal"** Radio Caroline is to move from the southeast coast to the Irish sea and seek a new audience in the north of England, Northern Ireland and the Isle of Man. Radio Atlanta is to stay off the east coast and be renamed Radio Caroline south.

Saturday 4 — **"Egg Hardship"** People living on small incomes have suffered following the Egg Marketing Board's decision to withdraw cheaper, second quality, eggs from the market.

Sunday 5 — **"Guided Missile Ships"** Following the launch of HMS London, Britain's new guided missile destroyer, at Greenwich yesterday, the navy is to unveil two more next week.

Monday 6 — **"Coronation Street Back on Air"** All independent and national television stations have returned to work after the technicians' union called off their week-long strike.

Tuesday 7 — **"Mont Blanc Avalanche"** 14 experienced climbers have died after being swept up by an avalanche on the Aiguille Verte some 13,000ft up. Among the dead was a former French skiing world champion.

HERE IN BRITAIN

"Greyhound Betting Coup"

A betting coup was attempted at Dagenham Greyhound Stadium that might have cost bookmakers over £10 million. There was only *one* winning ticket for the 4.30. At the track, the Tote windows were blocked with scammers making 'unlikely bets' – stopping others from betting on the favourites - and 10 minutes before the race, all the telephones went dead for half an hour.

Because of this, "bookies" all over the country could not *place* the many potentially 'winning bets' on the favourites that they had accepted from their customers. All wagers are to be refunded.

AROUND THE WORLD

"US Civil Rights"

President Johnson has signed the US Civil Rights Act of 1964, officially bringing the Act into fruition. In a triumphant speech to Congress, the President spoke of the time, some 188 years ago, when *'a small band of valiant men began a struggle for freedom with the writing of the Declaration of Independence'*.

That struggle, he said, was a *'turning point in history'*, and now, in a similar vein, this new act will ensure *'fair and equal treatment for all people in America and continue the ongoing process of racial desegregation across the country.'*

The Malcolm Clubs

The 21st anniversary of the RAF's 'Malcolm Clubs' is being celebrated this year with a number of stage shows, parties and other functions in all the clubs from Wittering in Britain to Singapore. Most clubs are in Germany and a special show from Rheindalen will be broadcast by the British Forces Broadcasting Service. There are currently twenty one clubs but at its height, the organisation had over 100 clubs in RAF stations across the world.

Malcolm Clubs get their name from Wing Commander Hugh Gordon Malcolm, a Scottish airman who was awarded the Victoria Cross, the highest award for gallantry in combat that can be earned by a British or Commonwealth soldier. After his death in 1942, the clubs were formed in his memory, and continue to support RAF airmen across the world. Malcolm became a commissioned RAF pilot in early 1937; following a near fatal crash in 1939, gaining a fractured skull, he returned to flying after four months of intensive care and it was here that he met his future wife, one of the nurses at the Princess Mary Hospital. During 1940, Malcolm, now a Squadron Leader, was part of the first night-time bombing campaigns of the war.

In 1942, Malcolm was posted with his squadron to give ariel support of the Allied invasion of North Africa, Operation Torch. Promoted to Wing Commander, he led the campaign flying the unsuitable Blenheim V's, sustaining heavy losses. This culminated in a raid on a German fighter airbase in December 1942, in Tunisia. The squadron was intercepted by enemy fighters and all of Malcolm's aircraft were shot down. His body was recovered and laid to rest in Tunisia, and the Wing Commander was awarded the V.C. posthumously in 1943. The medal now sits in the Imperial War Museum.

JULY 8TH - 14TH 1964

IN THE NEWS

Wednesday 8 — **"US Nuclear Ship in Southampton"** The mayor and the American Consul greeted the arrival of the US nuclear merchant ship the 'Savannah' when she docked at Southampton Port. The ship will be opened to the public during the visit.

Thursday 9 — **"UK's Share of Concorde Soars"** Britain's share of the development costs of the Concorde airliner have soared to over £140 million. This is an increase of more than 100% from two years ago.

Friday 10 — **"Mass Hysteria"** Screaming crowds of over 100,000 people lined the streets of Liverpool to greet the Beatles on their return home from their US tour.

Saturday 11 — **"Forth Bridge Accident"** Three steel erectors carrying out work on the Forth Bridge have been involved in an accident when the safety net, under where they were working, fell out from beneath them. One man is confirmed dead, one injured and the third, missing.

Sunday 12 — **"Choice of 2m Numbers"** A new subscription service for a worldwide telephone network linking over 200 million numbers has been announced. The system will direct dial into the international network with the need for no more than 15 numbers.

Monday 13 — **"Postal Strike"** Of the 12,500 post men working in the London area, over 10,000 have been on strike at the weekend. Workers returned today to deal with the millions of unattended letters that had accumulated.

Tuesday 14 — **"Stowaway Denied Entry"** A 15-year-old boy who hid onboard the Queen Mary at New York, in an attempt to reach Switzerland to visit a former school friend, has been discovered, and refused entry to land at Southampton. The boy's parents have paid the £160 ticket home.

HERE IN BRITAIN

"Prison Perks"

Thirty-five prisoners attended the re-opening of the Stratford-Upon-Avon canal after helping fast track the project by aiding in the repair work. They were allowed to stand within some 20 feet of Queen Elizabeth, the Queen Mother, as she cut the tape to reopen the canal.

The narrow boat 'Linda', in which she and high-ranking officials from the Services, stood, then moved off under an iron bridge, made in Wormwood Scrubs, to enter the river Avon. The National Trust said that *'without the help of the prisoners, the reopening would hardly have been possible so soon'.*

AROUND THE WORLD

"Snake Escape"

An explosion following a fire onboard a lorry carrying 13 tons of ammonium nitrate and two tons of dynamite, has not only killed six people, but also let loose a number of dangerous snakes from a nearby reptile farm at Marshall's Creek, a Pocono Mountain resort in Pennsylvania.

Rattlesnakes, Copperheads and Cobras were among those missing and people nearby are being warned of the dangers posed by the escapees. The lorry had blown two tyres and the driver parked up next to the farm and fell asleep, not noticing the fire break out.

THE ROYAL TOURNAMENT

1964
ROYAL TOURNAMENT

This year marks the tercentenary of the Royal Marines, whose marching band will be closing the Royal Tournament. Following the compression of the British Armed Forces into one central command under the Ministry of Defence, this year's tournament is somewhat trimmed down. The watchwords for the event, according to Major General Nelson, the coordinator, are to be *'speed and action',* and not just to avoid the overrunning and somewhat tedious moments of previous years.

The Major General has promised a shorter yet more punchy and exciting spectacle involving all three wings of the British Armed Forces and he was quick to dispel the fears that the combining and compression of the armed forces would lead to a removal of tradition. The highlights expected include the demonstration of free-fall parachuting drops by the Royal Air Force Paratroopers, and the Royal Navy's annual field gun competition, a pivotal element of the display since 1907.

The idea is said to have been born at a meeting of the National Rifle Association in the 1870s and the Tournament began as a series of skill at arms competitions, quickly evolving to include military bands and a variety of acts and displays. The inaugural display was held in 1880 and shooting, tug of war, tent pegging, tilting at the ring, sword v bayonet and lemon cutting were all present at what proved to a financially unsuccessful event. From there however, the show grew exponentially, with subsequent Tournaments attracting large crowds and it eventually relocated from the Agricultural Hall in Islington to Olympia in London, where it has been held ever since, only taking a brief hiatus' during the World Wars. Crowds still flock to see this demonstration honouring the best of the British Armed Forces in a great occasion of patriotism and military excellence.

July 15th – 21st 1964

IN THE NEWS

Wednesday 15 — **"MP Pay Rise"** The Leader of the Commons has released plans for an increase in MP's pay, by around £3000 per year. The plans are designed to be generous enough to avoid it becoming an issue in the future.

Thursday 16 — **"BOAC to Take 20 VC10's"** The Ministry of Aviation has to find money to compensate Vickers should BOAC only take 20 of the 30 VC10's ordered. The newly appointed chairman has decided that 30 new aircraft will be too much to handle financially.

Friday 17 — **"BP to North Sea"** British Petroleum are amongst the first applications for production licences for North Sea oil and gas from the Ministry of Power. BP has committed to spending over £5 million on North Sea drilling.

Saturday 18 — **"7 Hour Harlem Riot"** Police have been forced to open fire after a riot lasting over seven hours broke out on the streets of Harlem, New York. The violence stemmed from the murder of a black 15-year-old child by a police officer last Thursday.

Sunday 19 — **"The Shakespeare's"** Over 260 people sharing the name Shakespeare, gathered at the Shakespeare Exhibition in his hometown of Stratford upon Avon. The event has been called *'the largest family reunion in the history of British literature.'*

Monday 20 — **"One Million Cars"** Recent reports state that there are over 1.25 million cars in London alone, that are owned privately for personal use. These cars are said to make over 8 million journeys every day.

Tuesday 21 — **"Independent Malta"** Maltese independence is the expected outcome of the recently concluded negotiations between the British and Maltese Governments.

HERE IN BRITAIN

"Britain's Tallest Building"

The Minister for Public Building and Works was invited up to the top of the Post Office Tower and using an inscribed silver trowel, smoothed out the last of the concrete during the topping-out ceremony on Britain's tallest building.

The Minister was described as looking *'a bit out of practice'* as he gingerly looked over the edge of the building at the 600ft drop down to Tottenham Court Road. The Minister arrived at the top in the same lift used by the contractors, bringing a large crate of beer and a 'skip' of cement.

AROUND THE WORLD

"Kenyan Sorcery"

In a drive to remove sorcery from the country, the Kenyan African National Union has ordered over 200 witch doctors to hand over their potions and renounce their practices. The group, including 27 women, gathered at a public meeting in Baricho, where they confessed to practicing witchcraft and laid their tools at their feet, to be collected by Kenyan authorities.

One man confessed to the murder of over nine people *'by means of bewitchment'* and his promise to never *'practice again'*, gained a large cheer from the crowd of over 3,000 spectators who had gathered.

Harris Tweed In Court

The judge Lord Hunter has officially ruled that Harris Tweed must, and can only, be wholly produced by the islanders in the Outer Hebrides, and that no processing can be done on the Scottish mainland. The case has become well known amongst the Scottish people, turning out to be the biggest and costliest in the history of the Scottish Courts. Thankfully, the 345-page document recording the findings was not read in full by the judge, who instead gave a summary to the court. As per the stipulations of the 1934 definition of 'Harris Tweed', the product must be spun and dyed in the Outer Hebrides and, not only did the tweed finished on the mainland not conform with this, but it sometimes fell short other areas too.

The approval process of Harris Tweed is a lengthy one; there are many layers of checks and approval required before a Harris Tweed Authority Inspector will bestow a seal of approval upon an item of clothing. The stamp required takes the form of a Trademark Orb, and until such Orb is sewn into the clothing, it cannot be sold as official Harris Tweed. To this day, Harris Tweed is the only cloth that is protected by an Act of Parliament.

Up until the late 1800s, Harris Tweed was made entirely by hand out of the finest Scottish wool available. However, it wasn't until the exceptional weaving abilities of the 'Paisley Sisters' came to the attention of Lady Catherine Herbert that the company really took off. Lady Herbert commissioned the sisters to weave clothes specifically in the Murray family tartan, selling the clothes to the family as a bespoke set for their estate. From there, the word spread, and the Harris name grew to be the major player in luxury tweed.

JULY 22ND - 28TH 1964

IN THE NEWS

Wednesday 22 — **"No Mail Again"** Postal workers continue their official overtime ban causing havoc in letter and parcel delivery. It is thought that over 35 million letters await handling in the London postal area, with a further million in Birmingham.

Thursday 23 — **"The Queen and Her Marines"** The tercentenary of the Royal Marines central event involved Queen Elizabeth carrying out a ceremonial inspection of the 41 Commando unit. Many Commandos were understandably absent, as the majority are serving overseas.

Friday 24 — **"Post Office Bank Delays"** Over 500 people a day who bank with the Post Office are unable to get their money out in time for their holidays as their applications to withdraw more than £10 are being held up in the postal strike.

Saturday 25 — **"Strike Over"** The government has agreed to a 6.5% pay increase and the postal workers strike has been called off. The basic wage for postmen in inner London is £12 17s a week; elsewhere it is £11 15s.

Sunday 26 — **"Drug Test Concerns"** The Pharmaceutical Society of Great Britain is encouraging the Ministry of Health to set up an independent control body for testing drugs and other medicated products.

Monday 27 — **"Dartmoor Prison to Stay"** Following an inspection by the Home Secretary, the government has announced that due to overcrowding in other prisons and an increase in crime, Dartmoor will stay open for the foreseeable future.

Tuesday 28 — **"Winston Churchill Retires Aged 89"** *'The greatest member of Parliament of this or any other age.... The oldest among us can recall nothing to compare with his life and the younger ones among you, no matter however long you live, will never see the like again.'*

HERE IN BRITAIN

"Keep Britain Tidy"

In an appeal directed mainly at youths, people are being encouraged to join in anti-litter campaigns organised by the Keep Britain Tidy Group. Many youth organisations have lent their support to the campaign following the publication of a number of shocking statistics; last year over 6,000 cars were abandoned in the streets and *'countless more in the fields and woods'*.

Not only this, but it was estimated that during a single bank holiday weekend, over 20 million picnickers left behind 10,000 tons of litter, costing the taxpayer over £1 million to clear.

AROUND THE WORLD

"Poetry in Rapid Motion"

A computer has been programmed how to write poetry at a rate of 30 poems a minute but is expected to be capable of over 500 once its vocabulary is increased.

Although the poetry is far from amazing, the lines are at least readable. The program was designed by a Miami high school teacher who programmed in 15 nouns, 13 verbs in the past tense, 13 prepositions, 16 adverbs and 10 adjectival phrases. *'Silently the crystal fields floated against the deserted mountainside as the moon rose the serene landscape glowed darkly'* is just one composition.

The Proms

With a broadcast price of just one shilling (5p), the 1964 season of Henry Wood's Promenade Concerts should attract an, albeit virtual, audience of over 50 million.

There have been Promenade Concerts – literally, concerts where you can walk about, in London, for more than a hundred years and our present series can trace its ancestry to the entertainments in the public gardens of Vauxhall, Ranelagh and Marylebone in the eighteenth century. The original English promenade concerts at the Lyceum Theatre in 1838 were conducted by Musard and consisted of instrumental music of a light character, containing overtures, solos for a wind instrument and dance music (quadrilles and waltzes). The change from theatre to concert hall, Queen's Hall, was made by Robert Newman when, in 1895, he started the present series with Henry J Wood as conductor. Newman wished to generate a wider audience for concert hall music by offering low ticket prices and an informal atmosphere, where eating, drinking and smoking were allowed. He said, *"I am going to run nightly concerts and train the public by easy stages. Popular at first, gradually raising the standard until I have created a public for classical and modern music."*

In 1927, the BBC saw that the concerts would provide a full season for broadcast and fulfil the Corporation's remit to 'inform, educate and entertain'. After the Queen's Hall was bombed in 1941 the Proms moved to the Albert Hall where their policy remains, classics plus new works and among the established artists, promising newcomers. Nine orchestras have been commissioned for this year, including two chamber orchestras for the first time ever. The 26 conductors are being led by Sir Malcolm Sargent who shares a 70th Birthday with the Proms themselves, and Mr Basil Cameron will conduct on his 80th Birthday.

JULY 29ᵀᴴ - AUG 4ᵀᴴ 1964

IN THE NEWS

Wednesday 29 — **"US Moon Craft on Course"** The course of the United States Ranger VII moon rocket has been successfully altered so that it is heading for the light side, not the dark side, of the moon. The craft will take thousands of up-close pictures of the moon's surface.

Thursday 30 — **"Trapped Miners"** Nine miners trapped 200ft underground at Champagnole, in eastern France, for over four days are no closer to being rescued. Rescue teams were halted by possible further hillside movement making it too dangerous to continue.

Friday 31 — **"A Tremendous Technical Achievement"** President Johnson praised the Ranger VII mission whilst he viewed a collection of over 4,000 photographs, showing in more detail than ever before, the surface of the moon.

Sat 1 Aug — **"French Ship Mystery"** An unknown shipwreck has been found in the South of France, just off the Cape d'Agde. Dated by experts as over 3,000 years old it makes it the oldest shipwreck in French waters. Considerable cargo including copper, bronze and bracelets have been discovered in the hold.

Sunday 2 — **"Police on the Offensive"** Hastings police forcibly removed youths who have spent the weekend fighting and terrorising holidaymakers in the town. They marched the offenders three miles beyond town boundaries.

Monday 3 — **"Gentlemen Jim"** Pop singer Jim Reeves, along with his manager, has been found dead in the wreckage of a light aircraft 20 miles from his home in Nashville, Tennessee.

Tuesday 4 — **"Scapegoats"** Brick makers believe that they are being made the scapegoats of the ongoing brick shortage plaguing developers across the country. A spokesperson for the industry believes that developers are '*biting off more than they can chew*'.

HERE IN BRITAIN

"The Pushing and the Fearful"

A study of driving habits of British motorists show that most road users fall into one of two categories, either 'competitive', or 'non-competitive'. The 'competitive category' display 'aggressive' and 'pushing' tendencies, '*taking a positive pleasure in overtaking and become completely frustrated when overtaken*'. The 'non-competitive' are more likely to show 'fearful' and 'careful' driving characteristics '*not becoming involved in overtaking and his attitude to being overtaken may be 'good luck to him'*.' Many drivers change from being 'aggressive' in adolescence to 'careful' in middle age'.

AROUND THE WORLD

"Suction Pump Fishing"

A Russian fleet of over 150 boats fishing off Cape Cod in Massachusetts, is using a large suction pump to suck fish into their holds through a trailing pipe about 12" in diameter.

The actions are being investigated by the Federal Bureau of Commercial Fisheries, who are calling for a 200-mile limit to be placed off the US shoreline, to protect America's own fishing industry. Some of the Russian factory ships could haul in up to 40,000lb of fish in one sweep while American smaller boats would not catch that much in five days' fishing.

RAF To The Rescue

RAF rescue squadrons are experiencing their busiest summer on record. Known as one of the country's most efficient welfare services, the 400 personnel strong RAF rescue squadron has predicted over 400 individual rescue missions by the end of the year. Funded by the taxpayer, the service costs over £165 a flying hour for each aircraft but this is increasing year on year as more accidents are reported. Compared to the 1955 figures, which saw the service carry out just 130 missions, the increase has been attributed to people being given more opportunity to be reckless. Now, more than ever, people are happy to launch themselves from the British coast on small inflatable boats, go swimming in nothing but a pair of speedos and even use inflatable beds to go exploring in open water, ignoring or ignorant of the dangers involved.

Although the job may seem trivial for the RAF, and their operations could be better served elsewhere, the force values the roles very highly. The RAF employs fantastic training for rescuing stricken air crews in combat, and what better training could there be than the real thing! The service utilises more helicopters than the rest of the armed forces, as their manoeuvrability, hovering capabilities and vertical take-off makes them ideal for coastal rescues, but it was only recently that the RAF employed such machines. Previously, the force had to use RAF marine craft, which were far less efficient at land reconnaissance and slower to reach target areas.

The increased strain the British public are putting on the service is a cause for concern for many high-ranking officials, and it is chastening that in spite of their valuable work and the lives they save, the RAF rescue squadrons are some of the most underappreciated in the armed forces.

AUG 5TH - 11TH 1964

IN THE NEWS

Wednesday 5 — **"Eight Days Underground"** The nine miners who were trapped underground for 8 days at the Mont Rivel lime-stone mine at Champagnole, eastern France, have been brought to the surface.

Thursday 6 — **"The Death Zone"** A 19-year-old soldier of the east German People's Army escaped under fire from his comrades to the Federal Republic in Bavaria. Zigzagging through the 'death zone' along the frontier, he collapsed exhausted but uninjured. A total of 19,705 persons have escaped from the east to the west since the Berlin wall was built in 1961.

Friday 7 — **"Elephant Fossils in Essex"** Remains of two pre-historic elephants, lying directly on top of each other, have been discovered in a clay pit in Aveley, Essex. They are described as being in *'near perfect condition.'*

Saturday 8 — **"BBC Injures Six"** Six people, including four girls, were injured whilst filming for the Billy Cotton BBC series when a special effects piano due to break apart, shattered and hurled pieces of wood over a radius of 30ft.

Sunday 8 — **"The Cyprus Crisis"** The United Nations have called for a ceasefire vote after Turkish attacks by sea and air on the island of Cyprus began.

Monday 10 — **"More Costly Smoking"** The cost of smoking has been increased by another penny; the second price increase this year. Tobacco companies blame the government.

Tuesday 11 — **"Flying Pope"** For the first time ever, the Pope has attended the Feast Day of Corpus Christi by helicopter, becoming the first Pope to travel by air. Pope Paul VI flew to Orvieto, where the Feast Day has been held since 1264.

HERE IN BRITAIN

"Whose Coins in a Fountain?"

Three students have pleaded not guilty after they were caught taking pennies from a water fountain in London. A policeman found the trio with their hands deep in an ornamental pond round a fountain at Marble Arch, arresting them for theft as *'the money belongs to the Westminster City Council'*.

Although the clever retort by one, *'well why do the council keep their money in a public fountain?'* may have not amused the Police officer, the magistrate advised them to plead not guilty to the charges. However, the three were later found guilty of theft.

AROUND THE WORLD

"New York Bear"

A large black bear was found roaming the suburban streets of New City, a town 25 miles from Times Square. Except in mid-winter, bears seldom venture into the suburbs of New York City and they are rarely spotted during the summer months, let alone seen walking along the pavement.

The bear reportedly was too tempted by the lure of ripe raspberries growing in many families' gardens, and the freshwater trout in the towns central brook. Whilst it would seem a matter for the police, they are powerless to intervene unless the bear *'becomes a menace'*.

DOME OF THE ROCK

The annual Dome of the Rock ceremony at the most sacred Muslim structure after the Ka'ba in Mecca, took place with several representatives from Arab countries and religious officials in attendance. The Dome of the Rock is the shrine at the centre of the Al-Aqsa Mosque compound on the Temple Mount in the Old City of Jerusalem and celebrates eight years since its restoration and renovation began. The ceremony was opened by King Husain of Jordan, the man who brought the restoration of the Mosque about. In 1954, the King launched a campaign across many Muslim countries for money to help restore the building, raising over £500,000 and support from major Arab figures. The carpet was paid for by the late King Muhammad of Morocco, and the Egyptian government paid for the surveying and direction of what needed to be done.

The Mosque is named from the outcrop of rock situated underneath the buildings' octagonal roof, from which, according to Muslim tradition, the prophet Muhammad rode heavenwards on the back of Al Burak, his magical horse. Other Arabic tradition states that it was the same place that Solomon built his temple, though no archaeological evidence has ever been uncovered to support this.

Now, the Mosque is *'the jewel in the crown'* dominating the Jerusalem skyline. The exterior walls are painted with sixteenth century Turkish faience tiles, which were replaced with almost identical replicas in the renovations, and the words Surah Ya Sin, 'Heart of the Quran' are inscribed in Arabic across the tile work and was commissioned in the 16th century by Suleiman the Magnificent. The inside holds many sacred inscriptions from holy texts and is lavishly decorated with beautiful mosaics and marble. The site holds religious significance for Christians, Jews and Muslims alike.

Aug 12th – 18th 1964

IN THE NEWS

Wednesday 12 — **"Rope Ladder Escape"** Charles Wilson, a member of the Buckinghamshire Train Robbery Gang has escaped from Winson Green Prison after knocking a guard unconscious and escaping via rope ladder down the 20 ft prison wall.

Thursday 13 — **"Berlin Wall Anniversary"** Approaching the third year since the building of the Berlin Wall, the Social Democratic Party in West Berlin has called for an hour's silence to be observed between 8pm and 9pm.

Friday 14 — **"Petrol Train Blazes"** Twelve petrol wagons were overturned and burst into flames after a collision with a light engine outside Didcot station, Berkshire. Two other wagons in the 48-wagon fuel train also caught fire and the blazing mass stretched along the track before fire fighters arrived.

Saturday 15 — **"Nuclear Disarmament Ongoing"** Another setback occurred in the 17-nation strong nuclear disarmament talks, when the Soviet Union rejected the US proposal for a 'verification process' on all new weapons.

Sunday 16 — **"Imperialist Plot"** Russian President Mr Khrushchev has accused the US and Britain of an 'Imperialist plot' against Cyprus in their encouragement of Turkey to threaten invasion.

Monday 17 — **"Second Great Escape"** The second great prison escape attempt of the week was foiled by prison staff in Strangeways Prison, Manchester, who caught wind of an 'outside plot' to free Gordon Woody, jailed for his part in the Great Train Robbery.

Tuesday 18 — **"Record Attempt Failure"** A British expedition of 11 men from the Pegasus Caving Club in Nottingham abandoned their attempt to break the 3,681ft world underground depth record in the Berger pothole near Grenoble as they failed to locate a passage which would penetrate the record level.

HERE IN BRITAIN

"The Glorious Twelfth"

Many people will refuse to pay this week's meat prices because Wednesday, the 'Glorious Twelfth', is the start of the grouse season, when a brace will fetch around £2.

When shooting is well under way, old birds for casseroles may fall to as low as 5s 6d (28p) and as the season progresses, more people will buy grouse instead of beef or lamb. Every year thousands of people travel to Scotland for the season, especially from America and the Continent, where they can hire a moor for the season for about £750.

AROUND THE WORLD

"Early Marriages"

A Professor at Cornell University has reported that more women in the US marry at the age of 18 than any other age, and that the average age of marriage is dropping rapidly.

The report continues that, assuming all 18-year-old women have a baby, and then go on to have four children in total, the US population would grow at a rate of over 2 million a year. The Professor warns that merely decreasing the average number of children per family is much less important than postponing the age of marriage.

NEVER MIND THE WEATHER

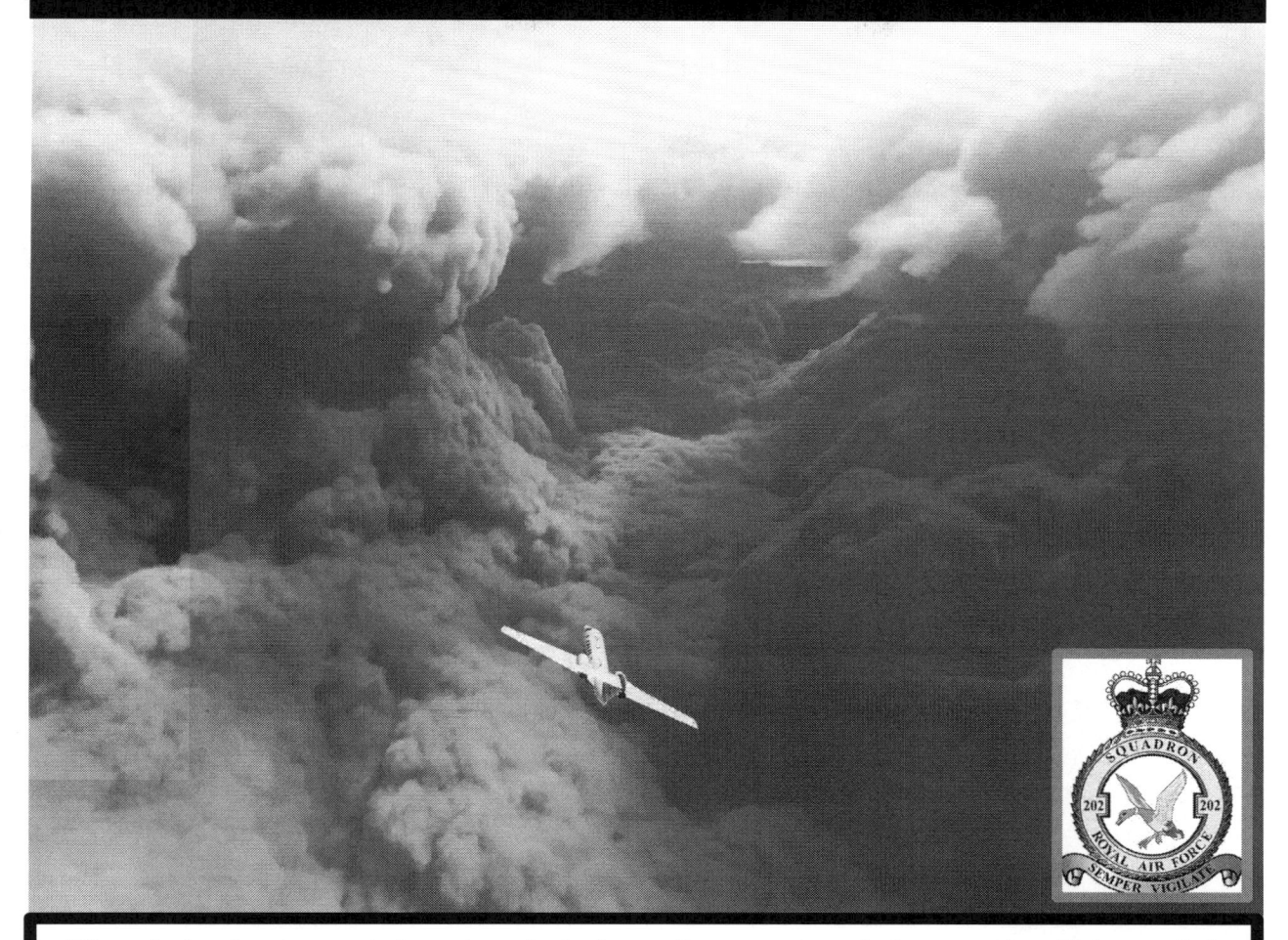

Although the developments in meteorological reporting serve to only increase the efficiency of air travel and effectiveness of weather reports, the advancements in technology has ultimately made obsolete one of the most pivotal of all RAF units. For the second time in its 50-year history, the 202 Squadron has been disbanded. For the past 18 years, the squadron has been making daily flights across the Atlantic, the North Sea and the English Channel to help put together oceanic weather reports for the meteorological service, and it made its last series of flights this week.

Born as the Number 2 Air Squadron of the Royal Navy Air Service, the squadron began its life flying over the sea and when adopted into the newly formed Royal Air Force, it mainly oversaw oceanic missions. The squadron was credited with three submarine sinkings during the Second World War. However, it is the Squadron's post war work which is most impressive; its motto *'Always be vigilant'* might as well have encompassed the song lyric *'never mind the weather'*, as this is what 202 Squadron was forced to do. Pilots were tasked to fly on extremely specific courses, at pinpoint altitudes, through whatever weather they encountered. Between 1945 and 1964, over 4,000 sorties like this were carried out, spanning what is estimated as over 10 million miles. Pilots were tested to the max maintaining course and height whilst completely blind of vision in cumulonimbus storm cloud. The most dramatic of moments came when, in 1957, a former Czech, turned RAF, officer flew straight through hurricane Carrie, a storm so bad that it caused the sinking of a German naval training ship. The information gathered by the young pilot proved to be invaluable in understanding and predicting future hurricanes.

AUG 19TH - 25TH 1964

IN THE NEWS

Wednesday 19 — **"Olympic Satellite"** The United States has launched a 'Syncom' satellite which, according to experts, should allow all corners of the world to be able to see the broadcast of the Tokyo Olympics later this year.

Thursday 20 — **"Royal Cows"** The Queen Mother has fulfilled a lifelong ambition to own a herd of pedigree Aberdeen Angus Cattle. She has bought two heifers and two cows for her privately owned 120-acre farm at Caithness.

Friday 21 — **"Crash Landing"** The new BAC one eleven has crash landed during a test flight on Army ranges near Salisbury. The pilot brought the plane down safely and none of the five crew onboard were injured.

Saturday 22 — **"Olympic Torch Kindled"** In Olympia in Greece, an olive branch was lit from the sun's rays focused by a concave mirror and the Olympic torch kindled. It will now be transported by 340 athletes to Athens, where it will make the journey to Japan by air.

Sunday 23 — **"Record Drunk"** Britain has broken its record of British adult beer consumption. At an average of nine glasses per person, per week, this puts the country fifth in the global rankings with Germany at the top.

Monday 24 — **"100 Nations United by Red Cross"** The internationally recognised symbol of a red cross as the emblem of medical services on the battlefield is 100 years old today. Over 100 nations, including all the great powers, adhere to the now famous symbol.

Tuesday 25 — **"No Need to Fear"** To put to rest Union's fears about increased automation removing jobs, the Ministry of Labour has forecast an increase in need for manpower in almost every industry over the next 10 years.

HERE IN BRITAIN

"Bathing Caps for Beatle Hair"

Glasgow City Council has announced that boys and men donning a 'Beatle style' haircut will be forced to wear bathing caps in the city's public swimming pools. The trend of 'mop head' youths could pose a risk to hygiene in communal baths, and hair clogs up the pool filters.

There have been complaints from girls who have to wear bathing caps, about male bathers with longer hair than their own but it will be left to the discretion of the staff on duty as to who *'is badly in need of a haircut'*!

AROUND THE WORLD

"Pampered Pets"

According to a report published in the Wall Street Journal, the people of the United States spent more last year on dog food than baby food. The actual figures come out at just over 50% more at no less than $530 million (£189m) and the figure for feeding American cats is an extortionate $125 million.

It is estimated that there are over 260 million dogs, 20 million cats and between 15-20 million birds kept as pets across the country, a figure that counting dogs alone totals more than the population of the US itself.

BARTLEMAS DAY

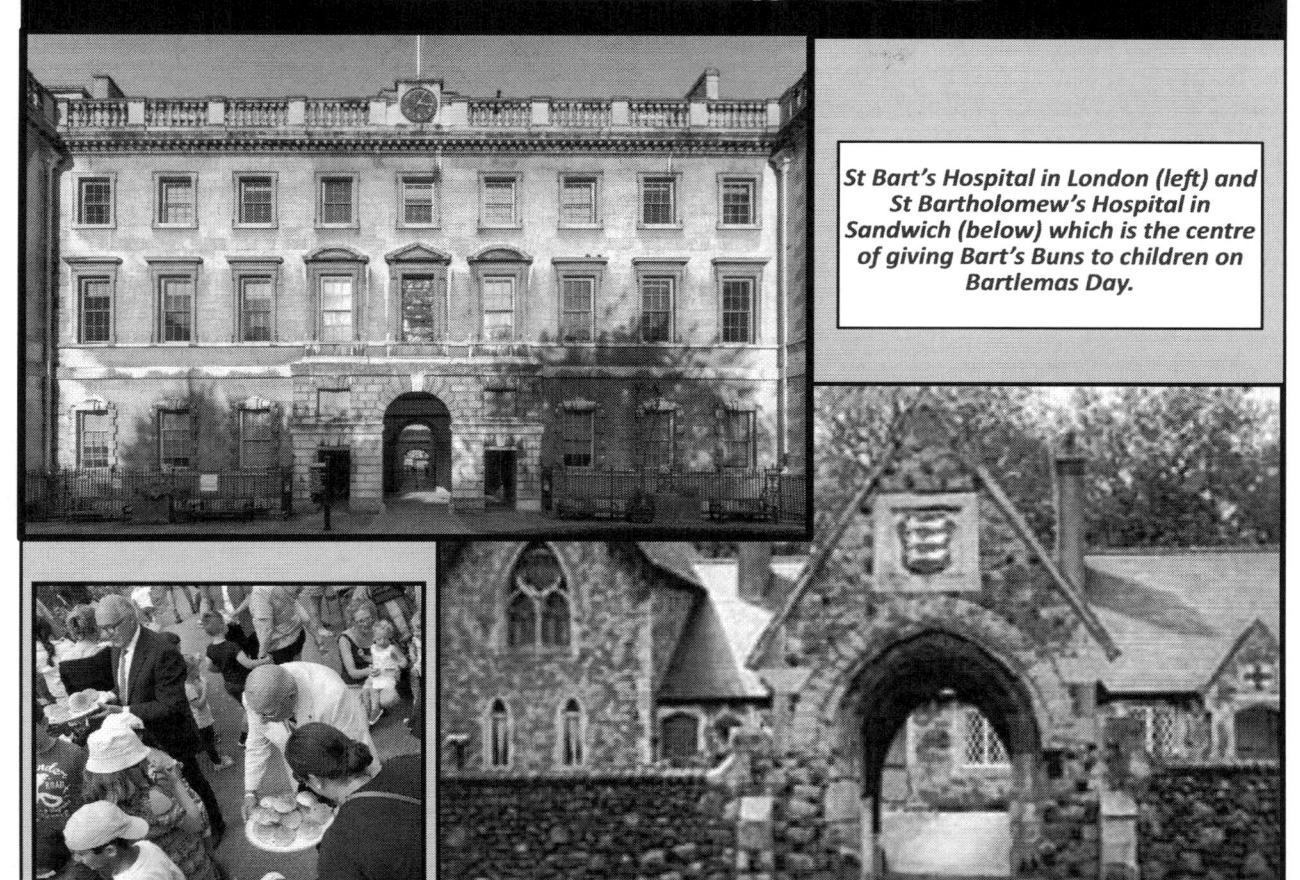

St Bart's Hospital in London (left) and St Bartholomew's Hospital in Sandwich (below) which is the centre of giving Bart's Buns to children on Bartlemas Day.

Saint Bartholomew was supposedly martyred by being flayed alive and this connection has made him the patron saint to butchers and tanners and by extension to bookbinders, for one of their traditional materials for binding books is leather. The Saint is best associated with two institutions, St Bart's Hospital in London and the ancient St Bartholomew's Fair. However, the Cinque Port of Sandwich in Kent also celebrates St Bartholomew's Day each August 24th. Among the most cherished institutions of the town is their St. Bartholomew's Hospital, not a traditional place for the sick, but a tranquil setting for the aged men and women of the town.

The records of the hospital give full details of its foundation in the reign of Richard the Lionheart, who landed at Sandwich on his return from the Crusades. There were four founding knights, and one of them, Sir Henry de Sandwich, has his tomb in the chapel of the hospital. These knights gave their land to provide a home for maimed mariners and the poor and elderly of the city to end their days in peace, and for more than 750 years, the 'brothers and sisters,' chosen by town worthies have lived on this same quiet site.

About 50 years ago the old hospital building of the middle ages was replaced by a quadrangle of little cottages, each standing in its garden with the ancient chapel, with its Norman arches, remaining in the centre. A service is held in the chapel on Bartlemas Day following which, the children of Sandwich run round the chapel and receive a current bun from the trustees of the hospital. The adults who attend the service are presented with a less edible 'St Bart's biscuit', a wafer stamped with the arms of Sandwich and the legend of the foundation.

Aug 26th – Sept 1st 1964

IN THE NEWS

Wednesday 26 — **"Biggest Sizzler for Years"** The hottest day for 11 years was experienced by East Anglia and London with temperatures hitting a high of 90 degrees Fahrenheit.

Thursday 27 — **"The Vice President"** At Andrews Air Force Base, before making the flight to Atlantic City, President Johnson has named Senator Humphrey as his choice for Vice-President.

Friday 28 — **"Philadelphia Riots"** After days of riots, Philadelphia becomes the seventh city in as many weeks to experience violence against police over their treatment of ethnic minorities. 341 people were injured, including 67 policemen.

Saturday 29 — **"East German Amnesty"** 'Political motives' are thought to be the reason behind the freeing of 1,000 prisoners from East German communist gaols. Many of the men had been detained for over 10 years.

Sunday 30 — **"Weather Satellite"** The United States have launched a satellite, 'Nimbus', capable of taking 'excellent' photos of the earth and are hoping to give daily weather updates and surveys of the planet. The satellite is able to relay 2,000 pictures a day.

Monday 31 — **"Saved by the Flowers"** A time bomb, presumably intended for General De Gaulle on his visit to Toulon two weeks ago, was discovered when a plant pot near the entrance to the Mount Faron War Museum burst into flames. The bomb is thought to have been put out of action by excessive watering.

Tuesday 1 Sept — **"Hovercraft Trials"** Far East operations might suit the military use of hovercrafts perfectly, the Ministry of Defence has revealed. Trials are to be run using the machine on swamp covered lands in Borneo.

HERE IN BRITAIN

"Mobile Car Press"

The Scrapmaster PSC376, described by some as looking like a *'coffin on wheels'* should help Britain get rid of its unwanted and derelict cars. The manufacturers claim the Scrapmaster to be the largest mobile 'baling' press on the market and it is capable of crushing two large saloon car bodies in one crunch into a one-ton bundle in three minutes.

Motor car disposal is obviously a growing problem and this will be the first purpose built 'car crusher', and will be transported on trial around a number of towns by an articulated trailer.

AROUND THE WORLD

"Crime Solving Computers"

US Police departments across the country are using computer programmes to not only help them solve crimes, but to also anticipate them happening. New York, Chicago and Detroit, have installed the equipment.

Each device costs in the region of $300,000 and is a valuable tool used mostly for statistical processes and identifying people, including those with criminal records. It enables the police to check quickly the antecedents of suspects without having to go laboriously through fingerprint files and the like. The computers require 19 police and 26 civilians to operate.

The Great Steam Fair

Shottesbrooke Park, in White Waltham, Berkshire was the 100-acre site chosen by Mr John Smith to host a 'Great Steam Fair' to celebrate the silver jubilee of the Friendship Circle of Showland Fans. The fair brought together half a century of fairground rides into one fantastic event. All of the rides and stands were powered by steam engines, ranging from old to modern, and the whole show was designed as *'a nostalgic exhibition, organised for adults, by adults.'* Mr Smith believes that old fairground rides are spectacles that should be enjoyed by the whole family, unlike the modern, fast paced roller coasters that are tailored to teenage adrenaline junkies. The Fair felt like stepping back in time.

The rides themselves, looked as if they had not aged a bit, and instead were as polished as when they were first set up, which was in some cases, over four decades ago. They move slowly enough for the riders to see and enjoy the elaborate paintings and carvings and are a joy to watch. Wherever they go, they attract crowds who just stand and stare. The steam-generated fairground organs, beautiful to look at, grinding out old-time music are very different from today's normal loudspeaker output. These beautifully elegant rides included a horse drawn fire-engine, a Venetian style gondola, and a 'steam yacht' swing, capable of carrying 40 people in each of its two cars and which provided the most fast paced excitement you could expect from the lazy, elegant fair.

The event was so well organised and advertised that it attracted locals, enthusiasts and showfolk alike, all of whom enjoyed a day out as if they had stepped back 30 years. It even drew attention from a company of filmmakers, who have made a documentary recording the event.

Sept 2nd - 8th 1964

IN THE NEWS

Wednesday 2 — **"Anglo-French Missile"** Britain and France are to conclude an agreement for the joint production of a new missile to be fired by British TSR 2 and French Mirage IV aircraft. The missile will use a new television guidance system and could be fired from aircraft at surface targets some miles away.

Thursday 3 — **"Channel Crossings by Liner"** P&O Orient Lines are now to offer channel crossings from £5 a time on their big ocean liners. Their fleet of 11 passenger ships will be making regular calls at Le Havre and Flushing to pick up the growing number of Continental passengers for Australia, the Pacific and the Far East.

Friday 4 — **"Forth Road Bridge"** The Forth Road Bridge has been opened by the Queen. A coastal mist which had concealed it since daylight, partially cleared just before the ceremony.

Saturday 5 — **"Driving Test Backlog"** Over 100 more driving examiners are to be recruited by the Ministry of Transport to clear the backlog of 400,00 people awaiting driving tests. Over one million tests having been carried out already this year.

Sunday 6 — **"Jet Noise with Bingo"** Bingo will be played at five sites around the Farnborough Show airfield for scientists to record how concentration is affected by aircraft noise.

Monday 7 — **"No More Park Radios"** The government has announced a ban on radios and musical instruments in London's royal parks following protests lodged by hundreds of nearby residents.

Tuesday 8 — **"Mail Order Pornography"** Scotland Yard have discovered over 73 firms selling mail order pornography, largely made in the US, in violation of the brand new Obscene Publications Act, 1964. 1,850 prosecutions are being considered.

HERE IN BRITAIN

"No Cycling on Forth Bridge"

Just before the opening of the new Bridge, the Cycling Tourists Club has complained that the footpaths and cycle ways alongside the road across the bridge would not be ready in time for the official opening by Her Majesty Queen Elizabeth.

It will be several weeks before the bridge will be opened for pedestrians and cyclists and as the existing ferry service will be stopped immediately on the opening, non-motorists have been left wondering how they will get across the river. The CTC were told that cyclists should pay to put their bikes on the train.

AROUND THE WORLD

"14-Year-Old Channel Swimmer"

An American schoolgirl from California has become the youngest girl to swim the English Channel. Leonore Modell, aged 14, made the trip from Grez Niz to Dover in just 15 and a half hours.

Subject to confirmation, the time and age breaks the previous record, held by Claudia McPherson, aged 17, of Canada, who swam in a time of 17 hours. Despite strong tides and a jellyfish sting, Modell arrived at the shores of the Dover cliffs in good spirits watched by crowds lining the cliff tops to support and cheer the young girl.

HE WHO MAKES THINGS SPROUT

The Aztec rain God, Tlaloc, translated literally as 'he who makes things sprout' has caused controversy and sparked the interest of many Mexican people after it was revealed by the Mexican government that his statue would be moved from his sacred resting place, where he has remained for centuries, to the site of the new National Museum. Many of Tlaloc's supporters and devotees are angry at the statue's removal and have foretold many disasters in the coming months. The people of Coatlinchan, where the statue was moved from, have predicted his moving is the cause of *'torrents of rain and floods'* in the poor areas of Mexico. Many came to watch the statue be taken away, and although having been persuaded to put national pride before local, they watched the god's departure with sullen faces, only brightening when they were placated by offers of new village amenities such as a school and a clinic.

The statue dates back to the early 16th Century, and stands 27 feet tall, weighing 167 tons. It is the tallest statue on the Continent and required a 72 wheeled trailer, pulled by two 600hp tractors and pushed by a 220hp bulldozer to maintain an average speed of just 2 miles per hour. As the cortege entered Mexico City with the god, strapped down *'like Gulliver by the Lilliputians'*, telephone and electric cables had to be cut and later replaced, to allow sufficient headway.

Tlaloc's following began during the time of the Aztec's who inhabited Mexico between the 14th and 16th Centuries. Five months of their 18-month ritual year were dedicated to Tlaloc, children were sacrificed to him on the first and third months and the rain priests ceremonially bathed in the lake during the sixth to obtain rain.

Sept 9th - 15th 1964

IN THE NEWS

Wednesday 9 — **"Whites Stay Away"** Prince Edward County, Virginia, which closed its public schools five years ago to avoid desegregation, reopened them, but only three of the 1,600 children who attended were white.

Thursday 10 — **"Christmas Card Calamity"** A range of personal Christmas cards has been launched by the commercial firm Valentine & Sons, designed to benefit six charities; however, the charities themselves now fear their own cards will not sell.

Friday 11 — **"Trail of Havoc"** A national disaster has been declared after Hurricane Dora struck the coast of Florida. The storm has spread havoc over 100,000 miles of land.

Saturday 12 — **"Families Flee"** 11 children and 3 adults successfully smuggled themselves across the East German border into West Germany by hiding in a lorry full of pig carcasses.

Sunday 13 — **"Scottish Circuit"** F1 World Champion Jim Clark is among the directors of a new racetrack that will be built just outside Edinburgh. The track will be just under one mile long and Scottish racing fans are delighted by the news.

Monday 14 — **"Souvenir Stalactite"** A coach driver admitted in court in Somerset, that he had broken off a priceless 42,000 year old stalagmite in Wookey Hole caves because he wanted a souvenir for a party of schoolchildren. He was fined £50 with 15 guineas costs.

"Biplane Crash" A Bristol Bulldog biplane crashed during the preliminary flight before its display at the Farnborough Air Show. No one was injured.

Tuesday 15 — **"General Election"** Prime Minister Sir Alec Douglas-Hume has called for a General Election on 15th October and the dissolution of Parliament on 25th September.

HERE IN BRITAIN

"Men in Colour"

The controversial 'Panda Crossings', which have been trialled for the last two years have been dropped. In their place will be a crossing with a red silhouette of a standing man and below it a green silhouette of a walking man.

When a pedestrian presses the button, the lit up red man will be replaced by a green man, signalling to the pedestrian that the road is safe to cross. For the motorist the crossings will have ordinary traffic lights. There are to be 90 crossings implemented for a six-month test.

AROUND THE WORLD

"Ashes Stay in England"

Although Australia won the Ashes this year, the priceless urn will remain in England and not be flown out to an exhibition in Sydney later this month. Instead, a replica urn will be used to commemorate the Aussie's victory over England in the cricket.

It has been revealed that the Ashes have in fact, never left England due to safety concerns, and remain at Lords Cricket Ground all year round. Other exhibits will however be on display, including the scorecard from the 1882 match, where Australia won for the first time.

CRAWLING TO GOLD

Swimming has been appearing in the news more and more frequently this year as the 1964 Tokyo Olympics draw ever closer, but swimming had not progressed as a sport for quite some time and it wasn't until the *'very un-European'* notion of front crawl came into force as an efficient form of swimming, that significant inroads were made. The Times gave a scathing account of the technique, when reporting on a race between two North American Indians and an Englishman in London 1844. Because the Englishman, adopting the graceful breaststroke, won with ease, little attention was given to the overarm splash *'lashing the water violently with their arms like the sails of a windmill and beating downwards with their feet with force'*.

However, this technique was used by Greeks, South Sea Islanders and Australian aboriginals hundreds of years before and evidence shows that even the ancient Egyptians used the overarm style to traverse the Nile in 3000BC. Now, the 110-yard world record is held by R. McGregor, who adopted the 'modern crawl', and the movement is considered to be the fastest way to move through water.

The English Channel record has 'rightly' returned to Britain, who although not optimistic about their chances of a gold medal at the Tokyo Olympics, are nonetheless proud to maintain the Channel time. The 'rightful' nature of the record belonging to England comes from the story of Captain Matthew Webb, who, in 1875 became the first man to officially make the crossing. And yet there are stories of an Italian, captured by the English from the Napoleonic forces at the Battle of Waterloo, who supposedly escaped from Dover and swam the Channel by dark to reach the coast of France.

Sept 16th – 22nd 1964

IN THE NEWS

Wednesday 16 — **"Brighton Marina"** Plans have been unveiled for the *'finest yachting marina in Europe and possibly the world'* to be built in Brighton in a £9.5 million scheme. The harbour will be capable of housing 1,750 yachts up to 150ft in length.

Thursday 17 — **"General Election"** Over 1,700 candidates are prepared for the General Election, with the Conservative and Labour parties standing for almost every seat; the Liberal Democrats have 360 candidates and 36 members of the Communist Party will also participate.

Friday 18 — **"London Panda to Moscow"** London Zoo authorities have said that they are willing to send their £12,000 giant panda, Chi-Chi, to Moscow to be mated with the Russian male An-An. Outside China these are the only giant pandas in captivity.

Saturday 19 — **"In Memory of the Few"** To celebrate the 24th anniversary of the Battle of Britain, over 750,000 people visited 12 Royal Air Force Stations which had opened their gates to perform air displays and memorial flypasts.

Sunday 20 — **"Penny a Day Keeps the Doctor Away"** On average, a British person will spend at least a penny a day on NHS medicine. This statistic comes in comparison with the average of 5d (2p) a day on beer and 3.5d (1.5p) on cakes.

Monday 21 — **"Continental Shelf Oil"** Britain has become the first North Sea country to permit a full-scale search for oil and gas after granting licences to 22 major oil companies.

Tuesday 22 — **"Dartmoor Escape Playground"** A further four violent inmates successfully made their escape from Dartmoor Prison. Only one is yet to be recaptured, but this escape attempt marks the 30th from the prison in the last three years.

HERE IN BRITAIN

"Filling the Moat"

Police have been forced to deal with students attempting to fill the moat of the Tower of London with water from the River Thames after they stormed the Tower with buckets to publicise their 'rag week'. They said they were filling the moat to celebrate *'Oliver Cromwell's historic swim in it'*.

Over 130 students and their girlfriends from Farnborough Technical College and the Royal Aircraft Establishment arrived at the Tower on three packed coaches wearing fancy dress. The students claimed that *'victory is ours'* before boarding their coaches and returning home.

AROUND THE WORLD

"10,000 Mile Drift"

American author and famous marine explorer, William Willis, has arrived in Queensland Australia after drifting over 10,000 miles on his raft across the Pacific Ocean. Having started out from Peru in July 1963, Willis injured his back at the beginning of last month, paralysing him from the waist down for six days, but nonetheless completed his journey on a 31ft steel raft.

The 71-year-old embarked on the adventure to prove that age was not a limiting factor, and can't wait to return to America where he plans to lecture about his travels.

INSECTS OF CLIMATE CHANGE

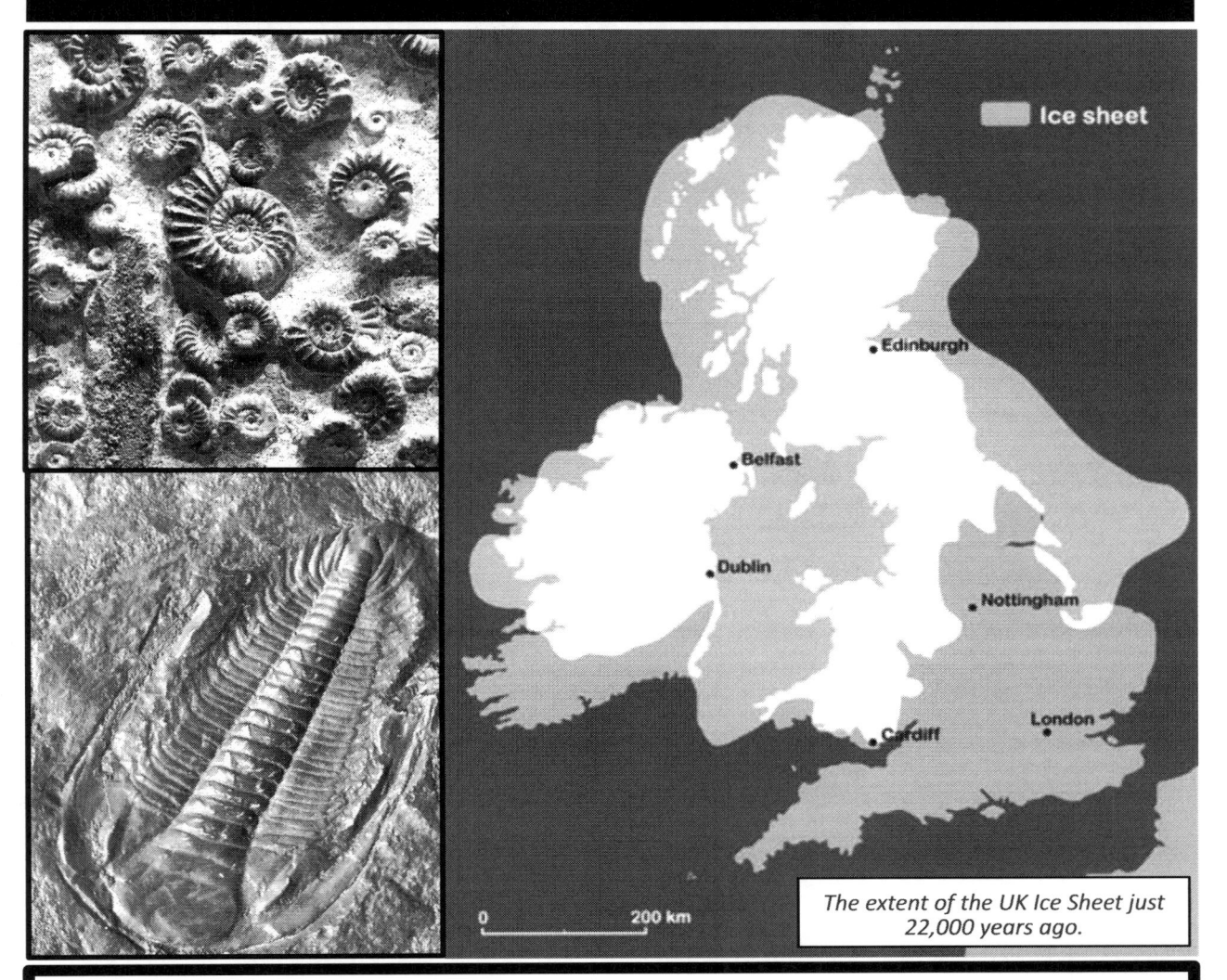

The extent of the UK Ice Sheet just 22,000 years ago.

The changes undergone by Britain's climate during the past 100,000 years is no better recorded than through insects, insect remains, insect populations and tree bark, according to a new study by Professors at Birmingham University.

The report shows that beetle fossils, specifically, were a great indicator of climate change, as they only lived in optimal conditions, conditions that remain the same to this day. Samples were taken from very well preserved remains under Trafalgar Square, Ipswich, two sites in Worcestershire and from a sand quarry in Cheshire. The beetles were typically fastidious about temperature and living conditions, so that a change of a mere 1.5 degrees centigrade on the average for a summer month could be enough to eradicate the species from an area, or on the other hand, see a dramatic increase in population.

The Professors also described elaborate tests carried out on the mysterious 'Sausage tree', native to Uganda, which grows 12lb fruits at the end of long stalks in just one month, and these showed them there had been no detectable evolution there during a period in which the British climate changed from being warm enough to support the hippopotamus to the intense cold of the ice age. Using data like this, they say, meteorological sites could predict future climate tendencies, and thus taper economic calls appropriately.

Sept 23rd – 29th 1964

IN THE NEWS

Wednesday 23 — "Royal Opening for Nuclear Station" Hunterston, the most powerful nuclear power station in the world, was opened by the Queen Mother in Scotland watched by 2,000 people shivering in the covered stands as wind and rain lashed the Ayrshire coast.

Thursday 24 — "Port Galore on A4" A lorry carrying over 1,400 gallons of port was involved in a crash on the A4. One cask rolled off and port spilt over the road. Five more casks sprang leaks. Passers-by were queuing to collect the drips in milk bottles and jugs.

Friday 25 — "Ship Traffic" A severe trade and labour shortage because of summer holidays and men's refusal since July to work weekends, has caused the Port of London, the *'worst period of congestion and delay since the 1950s'*.

Saturday 26 — "Accessible for All" Travel agencies are expecting a sharp increase in foreign holidaymakers from next year as they revealed a holiday can cost as little as £150. They aim to attract the mass market.

Sunday 27 — "TSR2" Britain's long awaited supersonic reconnaissance aircraft has made its maiden flight at Boscombe Down. The British Aircraft Corporation, who developed the aircraft for the Ministry of Defence, called the flight a *'a complete success'*.

Monday 29 — "17 for the Territorials" The Territorial Army will at last allow young men at the age of 17 to enlist, coming in line with the regular Army. The 17-year-olds will not be required to serve abroad.

Tuesday 29 — "New Lord Mayor" Sir James Miller at Guildhall was elected the new Lord Mayor of London, with the colourful pageantry of the ancient Michaelmas Day ceremony. Miller is a former Lord Provost of Edinburgh.

HERE IN BRITAIN

"Smoking Reduction"

In a survey of over 6,000 electors carried out by the National Opinion Polls, it has been revealed that half of the people aged 21 or over are smokers. This includes 67% of all men, and 36% of all women and smoking is particularly popular among those aged under 55 and the working classes.

However, whilst these numbers may seem high, there is a slight decrease from previous polls over the past few years. Social class, age and influence of parents are key contributing factors as to how likely someone is to be a smoker.

AROUND THE WORLD

"Tokyo Monorail"

The longest commercial monorail service in the world, running throughout Tokyo, has begun a six-minute shuttle service between the city and the Haneda Airport. The trains are capable of 65 miles an hour and cost 5 shillings per person, and a further 4 shillings for baggage handling.

The private venture will need to run close to capacity, shuttling over 100,000 people a day, in order to pay interest on the almost £20 million it cost the build. The monorail's main competition will come from the motorway, which boasts a 20-minute drive to the airport.

NAZI ART GALLERY

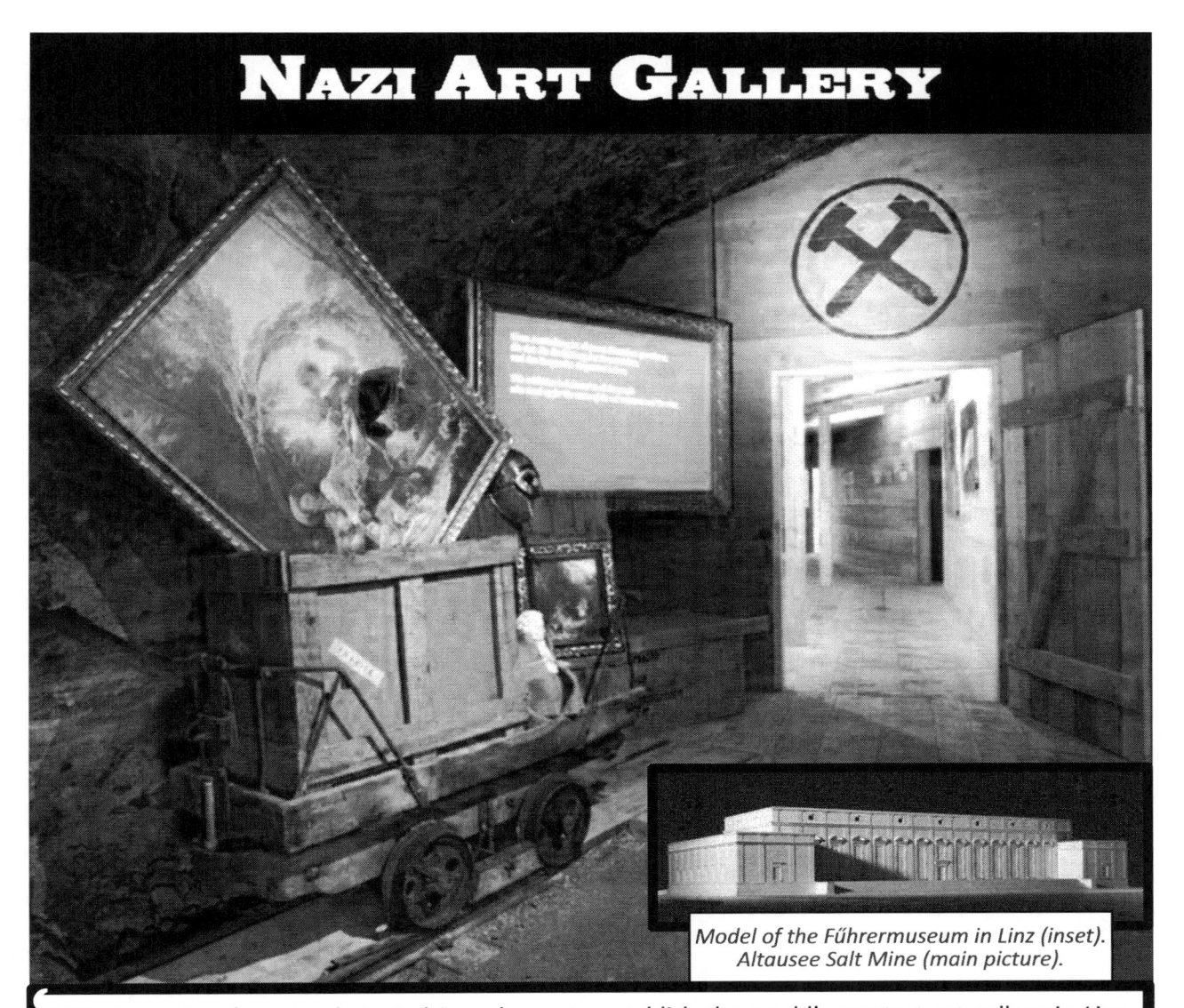

Model of the Fűhrermuseum in Linz (inset).
Altausee Salt Mine (main picture).

Hitler's passion for art culminated in a dream to establish the world's greatest art gallery in Linz, Austria, where he was born, and explains his obsession with collecting famous paintings, statues and tapestries from the countries he invaded. A report now declassified by the United States Government describes the extent of the German's plunder, even referencing an attempt to blow up some of the priceless artefacts at the end. Hitler stored his collection in an Austrian salt mine, from where much of it was sold on the black market to fund an underground Nazi movement after the end of the war. As such, many of the objects originally in the collection, stolen from national archives and museums, remain lost. The report, named 'Interrogation Report Number 4', was compiled through a number of interrogations with high-ranking Nazi officials by the Office of Strategic Services.

The 'Fuhrermuseum' as it was to be called, would have increased the population of Linz from 55,000 to over 5 million, and according to Hitler's eccentric plans, the railway line was going to be moved some four kilometres to accommodate the gallery. The glorification of German history played a large part in the art chosen by the Fuhrer and an organisation called the Sonderauftrag was set up to plunder the artworks. At its peak, over 5,000 paintings, 1,000 prints and a large collection of books, tapestries, statues and artefacts were collated in the Austrian salt mine, and the attempts to bring art, and with that, how people were allowed to perceive art, under the arm of the Swastika looked all but certain. Should the advancing American forces not have uncovered the mine, the art may have been lost forever, and with it, centuries of history and national culture.

Sept 30th – Oct 6th 1964

IN THE NEWS

Wednesday 30 — **"September Sun"** This month was the sunniest since 1911, with temperatures experienced more like June than the beginning of Autumn. Many towns experienced over 230 hours of sunlight across the four weeks.

Thursday 1 Oct — **"Berlin Passes"** After a fortnight's wait, West Berliners are finally eligible to collect passes allowing them to visit East German relatives the other side of the border. They are valid for one day during the fortnightly autumn period or over Christmas.

Friday 2 — **"Firebombs in Belfast"** Violence has broken out on a serious scale in Belfast, with crowds taking police days to disperse. Several were injured in violence between police and pro-republican protestors, and two police patrol vehicles were destroyed by firebombs.

Saturday 3 — **"More Calories"** Britain's food consumption has crept up a further one percent to 105% of the pre-war average. The increased availability of processed foods and the reduction of rationing are linked to this increase in calorie consumption.

Sunday 4 — **"Berlin Tunnel Breakout"** Fifty-seven East Germans successfully escaped through an underground tunnel to West Berlin before it was found and sealed by East German authorities. This is the highest number to escape en masse through the Berlin wall since it was erected in 1961.

Monday 5 — **"African Honours for Churchill"** Sir Winston Churchill has been made a Freeman of the small South African town, Escourt in Natal, where he was stationed as a war correspondent during the South African War.

Tuesday 6 — **"Slow Motion Baggage"** After strike action was voted out, dockers in Southampton were purposefully slow and inefficient in their handling of baggage in support of their rejected five-point pay claim.

HERE IN BRITAIN

"Tin Openers to Go"

Britain's largest supplier of tins, Metal Box, may have introduced the actual 'best thing since sliced bread' in the new Easy Open Tin, which has a tin opener built in, much like the lid of a fizzy drinks can. A tab fixed to the end of the tin, when pulled, tears a hole in the metal, allowing the lid to be pulled away.

This marks the end of a century-old uneasy marriage between the canner and the tin-opener. In 1830 a hammer and chisel were the tools recommended to the serious opener of tins.

AROUND THE WORLD

"Hyderabad Reservoir Disaster"

More than 1,000 people are thought to have drowned after a reservoir burst its banks just south-east of the Indian city of Hyderabad after 18 inches of rain had fallen in just three days. The town, with a population of 25,000, has been largely destroyed by the floods and was left sat in over 10 feet of water.

Authorities have said that at least 'several thousand' people were still stuck on rooftops and in tall trees and at least 100 of the sick and injured from the town's hospital are still unaccounted for.

REBELLIOUS YOUTH

Beach crowds take cover from battling Mods and Rockers
WILDEST ONES YET

A 'Scuttler' of the 1880s who was jailed (above).
Mods, with their scooters (left).

Whilst these days fervent youths are labelled with names like 'Mods' and 'Rockers', they are no different from the youths of the 1800s in anything other than name and age. Back then, rebellious youngsters in Manchester would have been named 'Scuttlers' and they were a major issue in the 1880s as they roamed around in 'Scuttling bands.' Violence between the bands was common and it is thought that the main appeal for the members, aged between 14 and 18, was to get into fights with others. Scuttling Bands consisted of anything up to 20 or so lads and were generally known by the names of the streets or districts from which they came. There were gangs from Ordsall Lane, Hope Street, Salford, Holland Street, Bengal Street and Pop Gardens, and there were the Grey Mare boys, and many more. Replace motorbikes, scooters and bike chain weapons with cutlasses, belts, and iron bars and the Scuttlers were almost a carbon copy of the 1960s Mods and Rockers. Hooliganism, as it was named was largely unsuccessfully dealt with by police, who were powerless to break up the fights, which often carried on for months at a time.

Scuttlers in the 1880s were easily recognisable by their distinctive clothing and trademark clogs and belts. The brass tipped boots meant that they were able to inflict maximum damage with their kicks. They also donned bell bottom trousers *'cut like a sailors',* flashy silk scarves and had their hair cut short at the back and sides, but long at the front; the hairstyle became known as a 'donkey fringe'. Tilted peaked caps were often worn to show off the fringe. The girlfriends of these hooligans were often out and about with their men engaging in whatever illicit activity was on the schedule for that day.

Oct 7th - 13th 1964

IN THE NEWS

Wednesday 7 — **"Commonwealth Immigration"** The Prime Minister made a speech to over 2,000 Yorkshire Conservatives where he spoke of the possibility of a flood of a million Commonwealth immigrants if the government had not legislated to control their entry.

Thursday 8 — **"Missing Prints"** French impressionist prints worth £2,000 have gone missing on their way to Dunfermline from the Victoria and Albert Museum. Earlier this year another exhibition from the V&A was mislaid on the way to the Carnegie Dunfermline Trust.

Friday 9 — **"Monte Carlo Rally"** The Monte Carlo Rally will start next year from London rather than Glasgow, as it has been for the past 33 years. The change comes after entrants dwindled from 61 in 1962 to just 31 this year.

Saturday 10 — **"Minimum Wage Rise"** The minimum weekly wage for adult male farm workers is to be raised to just over £10 a week from January next year. Nearly 500,000 people will benefit from the increase.

Sunday 11 — **"Multi-Man Spaceship"** Russia has launched a space craft with three men on board, a pilot, a doctor, and a scientist, to study how a group of specialists can cooperate over a long duration in a confined space. It becomes the first multi-manned space launch.

Monday 12 — **"Queen's Reception in Canada"** Her Majesty the Queen was welcomed by large crowds in Ottawa, Canada, when she laid a wreath during the ceremony for Thanksgiving Day.

Tuesday 13 — **"Jet-Powered Three-Wheeler"** The 'fastest man on wheels' title has been retaken by American Craig Breedlove, with a speed of 468 mph in the 'Spirit of America' across the Bonneville salt flats in his three wheeled jet powered car.

HERE IN BRITAIN

"Plastic Tank"

Experiments are ongoing at the Fighting Vehicles Research and Development Establishment in Chertsey for a new form of tank protection, which is expected to usurp iron armour plates. Light metals like aluminium are being compounded with plastics to create a remarkable vehicle that can still withstand high velocity tank guns but is also light enough to be transported via aircraft.

The primary aim has been to reduce weight without losing structural integrity. Britain operates the most powerful tank in the world, with a 120mm gun, but also the heaviest, weighing almost 50 tons.

AROUND THE WORLD

"Breathing Like a Fish"

The General Electric Company in New York has developed a new synthetic membrane with the properties of fish gills and human lung tissue. The new equipment is thought to have useful applications in underwater and space research, lung machines and oxygen tents. The membrane is made of silicone rubber just a thousandth of an inch thick.

In a demonstration, a hamster was shown sleeping in a box of membrane in a tank full of goldfish. As the hamster breathed, oxygen passed through the membrane from the water and carbon dioxide passed out as pressure increased.

The Tokyo Olympics

The first ever Olympic Games to be held in Asia are being held in Tokyo, Japan, between the 10th and the 24th of October. Originally, the intended Tokyo Olympics were those of 1940, but the games were moved to Helsinki after Japan's invasion of China and subsequently cancelled due to the Second World War. These games are also the first to exclude South Africa because of their apartheid system in sports.

Symbolically, the man who lit the Olympic flame, Yoshinori Sakai, was born in Hiroshima the day the atomic bomb was dropped by the US on the city and was chosen to be a physical representation of Japan's post war rebirth into an inherently peaceful nation. The whole event has been a major success for the Japanese people and culture, helping to showcase technological advancements but also accelerating community sports initiatives and infrastructure. The games were scheduled for mid-October to avoid the Japanese summer heat and the typhoon season in September.

The Games marked 'firsts' in several areas, both on and off the sports pitch. Judo, volleyball and women's pentathlon were introduced to the Games, fibreglass poles were used for pole vaulting, and it was the last Summer Olympics where a cinder track was used for athletics. The 1964 Olympics was broadcast live on television for the first time without the need for tapes to be flown overseas as they had been for the 1960 Games. Satellites were used to stream the games to the US and Europe and certain sports were filmed using Toshiba's new colour transmission system within Japan. Zambia became the first nation ever to arrive at the games as one country, (Northern Rhodesia) and leave as another, (Zambia) after declaring its independence the day before the Games' closing ceremony.

Oct 14th - 20th 1964

IN THE NEWS

Wednesday 14   "**Long-Awaited Success**" Mary Rand has become the first British woman to win a gold medal on the athletics track at an Olympic Games. She came home in first place in the long jump against a highly competitive field.

Thursday 15   "**Labour Victory**" In the closest General Election on record, a near dead heat, Mr Harold Wilson will be the youngest Prime Minister of the century to lead the fifth British Labour Government.

Friday 16   "**Nobel for King**" The Norwegian Nobel committee announced that the Nobel Peace Prize for 1964 has been awarded to Dr Martin Luther King in acknowledgement and honour of his efforts for peaceful solutions of racial problems in the United States.

Saturday 17   "**Naval Air Squadron to Go**" The Royal Navy's 'Outstanding Air Squadron of the Year', the 846 unit, is to be disbanded following the conclusion of its activities in Sabah, Far East Asia. The unit has flown over 3,000 operational sorties over the last nine months.

Sunday 18   "**New Man in Moscow**" Soviet Union Prime Minister, Nikita Khrushchev, has been replaced as leader of the Russian Communist Party and Prime Minister by Mr Leonid Brezhnev shortly following his 70th Birthday on the grounds of *'age and ill health'*.

Monday 19   "**Trawler Tantrum**" The detention of the 'Prince Philip Trawler' for eight days by Iceland has caused a protest by the British Trawlers Federation. The ship's Captain claims they were more than a mile outside Iceland's 12-mile radius when captured.

Tuesday 20   "**President Hoover Dead**" Former President of the United States, Mr Herbert Hoover, has died aged 90 at his apartment at the Waldorf Astoria Towers in New York.

HERE IN BRITAIN

"The Supercarwash"

Named the 'Supercarwash', Britain's first fully automatic car wash has been launched in London. The plant, which cost nearly £50,000, cleans a car in as little as three minutes using a fully automated process for the cost of 7s (35p). For bigger cars the charge is 9s (45p). American equipment and 10 men are used.

Cars are conveyed by an electrically powered guide track. Interiors are cleaned by vacuum hoses, outside dirt removed by steam guns, wheels automatically brushed, and at the same time, the body work is sprayed with warm water and light detergent.

AROUND THE WORLD

"Not Big Enough for Two"

For 15 hours, two women fought a 'tug of war' over the purchase of an English bicycle for sale on special offer, at a discount store in New York. Encouragement and food came from friends and family as neither woman dared to take her hand off the handlebars.

After being removed at closing time, the women returned the following morning, where the manager made them more comfortable with a pair of deck chairs. In the end, the shopkeeper sold the women two identical bicycles at the cut price of $10 (£3 1s 5d).

DONKEYS - VALUE TO VERMIN

Feral donkeys (left) descend from abandoned or escaped pack animals (above)

A six-week drive to kill up to 100,000 wild donkeys which are damaging valuable cattle grazing country in the far north of Western Australia is now well under way. The annual drive, organised by independent shooters and cattle station owners, has gained international recognition in recent years, and shooters from several countries have shown interest despite some animal lovers in Britain expressing concern about the possibility of donkeys being left wounded to die slowly.

The first three donkeys arrived in New South Wales in 1793 but they were not much used by Europeans who continued to use the horse as their main mode of transportation, only coming into wider use with the opening up of Central and Western Australia in the 1860s where they were extensively used until the late 1930s for freight haulage in areas where horse and bullock teams perished. Problems had also arisen when horses began to become sickened by some of the native poisonous plants. When donkeys proved to be resistant to these plants, more donkeys were brought in and when motorised transport took over, the teamsters - the men who drove the teams of donkeys - simply set their donkeys free, as they had no wish to shoot them.

Conditions were ideal for the donkeys to prosper in their feral (a wild animal that once belonged to a primarily domesticated species) state, as they graze all year round on grass, shrubs and tree bark, for 6 to 7 hours a day. This seriously affects the environment and produces many problems including polluting water holes with the potential to make native plants and animals extinct and, most importantly to ranch owners, the donkeys affect local agriculture, by over grazing pastureland, destroying fences and even infecting domestic animals with disease.

Oct 21st – 27th 1964

IN THE NEWS

Wednesday 21 — **"Blue Streak"** The second test firing of the British Blue Streak rocket has taken place in Australia with a *'perfect blast off'* according to Officials. The rocket flew directly on target hitting the impact area at Talgarno.

Thursday 22 — **"Literary Rejection"** Jean-Paul Sartre has confirmed that he will not accept the Nobel Prize for Literature. The explanation most commonly given has been his *'known aversion to literary prizes in general'.*

Friday 23 — **"Birth of New Town"** Cramlington New Town, already giving rise to over 15,000 new jobs and 12,000 houses, has officially been opened by the Duke of Northumberland. It is estimated that the town will have over 50,000 inhabitants at full capacity.

Saturday 24 — **"An Independent Zambia"** Northern Rhodesia, a former British Protectorate, has officially declared independence, along with the assumption of a new name, Zambia. The change marks the end of 73 years of British control.

Sunday 25 — **"South Georgian Expedition"** A 10-man expedition has left London to spend four months on the island of South Georgia in the Falklands. They will attempt to retrace the 1916 route of Ernest Shackleton after the loss of his ship.

Monday 26 — **"Open Act of Defiance"** Britain was accused by Mr Ian Smith, Prime Minister of Rhodesia, of 'blackmail and intimidation' after a warning of the consequences should a unilateral declaration of independence be made by the Rhodesian Government.

Tuesday 27 — **"New Fastest Man"** For the fourth time this year, the title of 'the fastest man on wheels' has changed hands again. American Art Arfos reached 536mph in his bright green jet powered car across the Bonneville salt flats in Utah.

HERE IN BRITAIN

"Good Samaritans Rebuffed"

The boys at a Secondary School in Lancashire are close to giving up on their 'good Samaritans' scheme. They offer their help in the evenings and at weekends to do chores and help elderly people, but they are being told to *'Clear off"* and having too many doors slammed in their faces.

The school's headmaster is bewildered by such a surprising reaction, even after trying to point out to the public that the boys were not asking for payment for their services, and he says it is no wonder the boys want to stop volunteering.

AROUND THE WORLD

"Women on Top"

A group of young Indian women have successfully scaled the 22,000 ft tall Mrigthuni peak in the Himalayas between Tibet and Nepal. They have become the first women to have even attempted, let alone succeeded, the climb. The group was led by Briton Joyce Dunsheath, who has a good deal of experience in mountain climbing throughout the world and Mrigthuni was selected as it was deemed to be *'not too difficult technically for women on their first major climb'*. Mrs Dunsheath led six Indian women, with ages raging from 18 to 31 and seven Sherpas.

INTERNATIONAL MOTOR SHOW

Record numbers of vehicle orders have been placed at the 49th International Motor Show being held at Earl's Court. Princess Margaret officially opened the show and orders totalled over £46 million within just a couple of hours. By the end of the second day this figure was up to over £250 million, £130 million of which comes from Ford sales alone. The ten-day event will see the showcasing of motoring brilliance from 12 different countries and is expected to be attended by over 500,000 petrol heads, many from overseas coming to see around 352 of the latest cars from Britain and other countries. Most of the cars on display are already on the road, and the motoring enthusiasts will be most excited to see the 'prototype' and development cars which are often brought out by manufacturers to encourage interest in their regular vehicles.

The star of the show is likely to be the new Austin 1800 'space saver', which is expected to get record sales as the only brand-new mass production car from the Big Five, this year. Austin's stand is dominated by a twin turntable carrying two models, one in sectioned form and the centrepiece of Triumph's display, is a white Triumph 2000 with gold-plated metalwork, the panels glinting from strategically placed lights above.

Many motoring fans come to the event to daydream of cars they would love to own, and find themselves sitting in V8 Chevrolet Corvettes, marvelling at the exquisite beauty of the Jaguar E-Type or dreaming of driving a Lotus Elan round a tight and twisty racetrack, making the event as much a fan showcase as an automotive sale - the biggest of its kind in the world, with British manufacturers given pride of place, the perfect place to showcase the best of British engineering.

Oct 28th - Nov 3rd 1964

IN THE NEWS

Wednesday 28 — **"Refined Welsh Landscape"** The worlds most automated oil refinery at Pwllcrochan, Pembroke, has been opened by Queen Elizabeth the Queen Mother. Extreme care was taken to conceal the works in part of the Pembrokeshire coast National Park.

Thursday 29 — **"Russian Research Ship"** The 333-ton Russian Research ship, the Zarya, has docked in the Pool of London, where it will stay for a few days before leaving on an Ocean studying mission in Norway, West Africa and Newfoundland.

Friday 30 — **"The University of the Air"** After Britain's first dedicated television tutorial course at Nottingham University five weeks ago, only 100 of the 1,500 students who signed up for the economics course have dropped out, a far lower number than expected.

Saturday 31 — **"Forecast Failure"** The Met Office are under fire for failing with their October weather forecasts. The forecast issued on October 1st missed the break from warm, sunny weather to rain, thunderstorms and gales and changeable weather.

Sunday 1 Nov — **"Veteran Run"** The largest cohort for many years have competed in the RAC commemoration run of veteran cars from London to Brighton. Only 13 of the 233 cars that left Hyde Park in the early hours failed to reach the finish line.

Monday 2 — **"200,000 To East Berlin"** With their new day passes, over 200,000 West Germans made the crossing to East Germany to visit family members during the first two days of the programme.

Tuesday 3 — **"Leaflet Drop"** Over 2.5 million leaflets have been dropped by British and Malaysian military aircraft over Indonesia, issuing a final warning to not engage in any more raids against the Malaysian peninsula.

HERE IN BRITAIN

"Selling Britain"

The Chairman of the Association of British Travel Agents has spoken of the Country's duty to 'sell' Britain to potential tourists. *'Britain's pageantry and traditions had great appeal, but why'* he asked, *'could not a ceremony like Trooping the Colour be staged at Wembley Stadium or the White City, where it could be seen by 10,000 people, instead of Horse Guards Parade where only a fraction of that number – most of them, privileged - could be accommodated? Why not cameras in the House of Commons, for people in the lobby to watch Parliament at work?'*

AROUND THE WORLD

"Olympic Coin Calamity"

All night queues for the new Olympic coins built up outside banks and post offices in Tokyo, as the demand for the 1,000-yen commemorative coins soared beyond all expectations. Over one million coins have been put on sale for foreigners, but the Olympic committee had severely underestimated the local demand for the remaining five million, all of which sold out within a couple of hours. An elderly woman has died from a heart attack in a queue in Osaka, whilst three men were injured by a car that struck another queue in Tokyo.

THE WINDMILL THEATRE

REMEMBERING Revudeville 1932 - 1964

A SOUVENIR OF THE WINDMILL THEATRE
Compiled by Jill Millard Shapiro

First opened in 1931, and becoming the centre of non-stop revue in 1932, London's Windmill Theatre is to be closed. The theatre's well-known slogan throughout the Blitz was *'We will never close'* but now, 33 years after its inaugural show, the curtains will close for the last time and whilst the traditional theatre, most recently owned by Sheila Van Damm, daughter of the founder, will go, the premises will reopen next week as a cinema.

Based in Piccadilly, The Windmill was founded by socialite Laura Henderson, a widow who inherited a fortune after the death of her wealthy husband, and her business partner and producer theatre impresario Vivian Van Damm and she managed to negotiate with the Lord Chamberlain to amend centuries-old laws to allow women to perform nude on the stage. With his permission, Windmill Theatre manager, Van Damm, began immediately to introduce by 1932 his *tableaux vivants*. Inspired by the Folies Bergère, nude or scantily draped women with the instruction *'if you move, it's rude'* were surrounded by elaborate moving sets while dancers whirled and wafted large feather fans. The feather fans used to conceal - or reveal - their nudity. The famous troupe of Bluebell Girls were favourite dancers at the Windmill. The troupe of precision dancers, all more than 5' 9" tall, were founded by Margaret Kelly, who was professionally called Miss 'Bluebell' to reflect her piercing blue eyes. From these motionless tableaux, the famous 'fan dance' was created.

The venue eventually evolved into the home of the variety show, where stars like Bruce Forsyth, Peter Sellers and Tony Hancock honed their acts, and although the girls remained the biggest draw, Spike Milligan, Peter Sellers, Bruce Forsyth and Barry Cryer were among those that had their first success at the Windmill.

Nov 4th - 10th 1964

IN THE NEWS

Wednesday 4 "Bus Trial" New electronic bus conductors are on trial in London for the next couple of weeks before their planned roll out to Manchester and Frankfurt on Main. The contraptions are small metal boxes, with 'ears and big mouths' designed to inspect the ticket of a boarding passenger.

Thursday 5 "Birmingham Ring Road" The next stage in the development of the Birmingham inner ring road scheme is for an almost 4-mile-long underground dual carriageway. Work is set to begin next year and will be completed in 1969.

Friday 6 "Himalayan Peak Climbed" The Himalayan Mountain, Thamserku, previously unclimbed, has been conquered by four New Zealanders from Sir Edmund Hillary's school house exhibition. The height of the mountain is 21,000 feet.

Saturday 7 "Margate Pier Fire" The 80-year-old pavilion at the end of Margate Pier has been badly damaged by fire. The building housed a café, bars and amusement slot machines which are used by thousands of holiday makers in the summer.

Sunday 8 "Remembrance Sunday" Whitehall was packed on the crisp sunny morning to observe the Queen place her wreath on the Cenotaph on the National Day of Remembrance.

Monday 9 "The Churchill Album" An album of records containing former Prime Minister Winston Churchill's most famous speeches is to be officially published for purchase by the Decca Recording Company. A large number have never been heard by the public.

Tuesday 10 "1812 Cannonball" A cannonball, thought to be one of those fired by the British at Washington USA during the war of 1812 has been found during recent excavations. The munition was taken to Fort Belvoir, Virginia, where it was detonated.

HERE IN BRITAIN

"DIY Brain Surgery"

Using only an electric drill and chisel, a doctor onboard the Northern Star Liner successfully carried out brain surgery on an injured crew member.
Steward John Bridgman had dived off a high balcony into the swimming pool, hitting his head on the bottom and necessitating the need for immediate surgery after falling deep into a coma. Engine room staff lent the ship's doctor an electric drill, which he used to perform a five-hour operation for severe brain compression. Mr Bridgman made a good recovery and was seen walking off the ship.

AROUND THE WORLD

"No Sugar"

Diwali, the happiest of all the festivals of the Hindu calendar, has been celebrated in a shroud of anxiety for the future this year.
It is a time for new beginnings and treats and a time for visiting, and the Hindu housewife who has no sweetmeats or drinks of sweetened milk or tea to offer, will feel she is not honouring Lakshmi, goddess of good fortune and abundance.
But sugar is scarce and to obtain enough just for the family, means long hours in queues or high prices on the black market.

REMEMBER REMEMBER

Guy Fawkes Day celebrations this year were particularly rowdy. By midnight, there were 98 arrests in Trafalgar Square. Seventy-two were accused of throwing fireworks, four of paddling in the fountains, 10 of insulting behaviour, one of obstructing police, four of assault on police, two of obstructing the foot way, three of threatening behaviour, and two of being drunk and disorderly. More than 40 teenagers were arrested after a 'pitched battle' between Mods and Rockers on Hampstead Heath and underground trains were delayed because of gangs of teenagers letting off fireworks. At Margate, police managed to contain a crowd of 800 young people who were watching fireworks on the seafront, until 300 ran off through the old town, causing chaos and smashing windows.

The nominal excuse for this annual celebration on 5th November, was the unsuccessful attempt by Guy, or Guido, Fawkes and a group of radical English Catholics to assassinate King James I by blowing up the Houses of Parliament. The plot went horribly wrong, and all the conspirators were executed. Catholicism in England had been heavily repressed under the reign of Elizabeth I with many priests put to death and Mass made illegal, so when the protestant James I came to the throne, the Catholic's hopes for change were high.

It soon became clear however that James did not support religious tolerance any more than Elizabeth had done, he condemned Catholicism as a superstition and ordered all Catholic priests to leave England. Hence the 'Gunpowder Plot' was hatched. Fawkes would light a fuse during the opening session of Parliament, James would be blown sky high, and he would escape by boat across the Thames. James's daughter would be kidnapped, installed as a 'puppet queen' and eventually married off to a Catholic thereby restoring the Catholic monarchy.

Nov 11th – 17th 1964

IN THE NEWS

Wednesday 11 — **"The Labour Budget"** The new Labour Government Chancellor has given his first budget, raising duty on petrol and increasing income tax by 6d, to 8s 3d in the pound from April next year. The changes will bring in over £200 million in tax to the government.

Thursday 12 — **"Ford Lead Rally of Britain"** Britain's BMC Minis have been eliminated from the possibility of winning the RAC Rally of Great Britain after the leading Mini crashed into a tree, and the second-place car retired with gearbox trouble.

Friday 13 — **"Lucky for Some"** The Pope has given away the 'triple crown' he was given by his old archdiocese when he became Pope. The tiara is valued at over £50 million and will go to benefit the poor.

Saturday 14 — **"Ford Strikes"** Eight British Ford plants have been hit by strikes following the announcement that 33,000 jobs would be made redundant. Only five plants remain open and 55,000 Ford employees are currently idle.

Sunday 15 — **"Concorde Simulations"** There is now enough data from the ongoing development of the Concorde programme to simulate flight trials and bring commercial pilots up to speed, quite literally, on supersonic air travel.

Monday 16 — **"MPs Pay Accepted"** Following advice from an external body, the Government has approved the increase in MP's pay to £3,250 per year. The average wage throughout Britain is £1,150.

Tuesday 17 — **"No British Arms to SA"** The export of arms from Britain to South Africa is to be banned by the Government as soon as existing contracts have been fulfilled. The contract to supply their air force with 16 Buccaneer aircraft remains under review.

HERE IN BRITAIN

"Plastic Grass"

Plastic grass for playing fields is the new plan by the Ministry of Public Building and Works, who have finished a number of tests and deem it *'playable'* for football and golf.

The plans have been met with some friction however, as rugby has not been deemed playable unless *'the players don't mind chewed up knees'*, and the Lawn Tennis Association have said that they have no interest in the product. The Ministry want to adopt the American model, of having playing fields of multiple surfaces.

AROUND THE WORLD

"Crate Flying"

A man has spent £345, considerably cheaper than a regular air fare, to mail himself from London to Australia as a piece of air freight. Reginald Spiers will be questioned by Australian customs officials tomorrow.

The crate he concealed himself in for 63 hours was 5 feet long, 3 feet deep and 2 feet wide, and was labelled as 'synthetic polymer emulsion' in the hope that no one would know what it was. Spiers did not take any food or water, and claimed that although he did not grow hungry, he was *'mighty thirsty'*.

Underground Classroom

A school environment is epitomised by the blackboard at the front of the classroom and the evocative noise as the chalk is scratched along the surface. A new school for miners, however, will not have a blackboard, instead they are to have black walls, as their training and learning will be completed in an underground tunnel little more than four feet high. Surrounded by coal, the unconventional classroom lies 600 feet below the surface in the heart of the Yorkshire coal fields.

Mining skills were traditionally handed down from father to son, but since the revolution in the coal industry, and the introduction of modern techniques, such practices have become too dangerous. A lot of the old physical ways that, in the old days, characterised the profession have been replaced with planning and brain power, and the 'hands on' use of a pick axe and shovel have been replaced with the operating procedure for a four-ton coal shearing machine. Each pupil in the mechanised section is accompanied by an instructor and the principal lesson is to absorb the massive list of safety rules from which, according to theory, all else will follow. The pit bottom galleries are carpeted with lime dust, *'it would absorb the heat of a coal dust explosion'*, and approaching the face, the gallery shrinks and pupils crawl on all-fours through a forest of hydraulic pit props, holding the 4' 6" high cut open *'like a long black jaw'*.

Recruiting has fallen over the past few years and the industry needs to make it clear that mining offers a career with good rewards, a secure future and sound training. However, new recruits will earn every penny of their 'good rewards', as one mining trainer said, *'It is not like working on a factory floor'*.

Nov 18th - 24th 1964

IN THE NEWS

Wednesday 18 — **"No More Rail Go Slow"** The Southern Region Motormen have decided to call off the train go-slow policy in place which has caused havoc with rush hour rail travel all week.

Thursday 19 — **"Football Coupons Seized"** Over 100 football pool coupons have been seized by American customs on their way from Bermuda to London after US officials deemed the coupons to be 'lottery tickets' and thus not legal to pass through the United States.

Friday 20 — **"Holy Disaster"** Just 10 days before the scheduled opening of a new £40,000 Catholic Church near Leeds, the roof has fallen in. In typical understatement, the parish priest said, *'This is a setback, unfortunate and unexpected, but we will carry on.'*

Saturday 21 — **"£22 For All Mothers"** All of Britain's mothers are to receive a £22 government grant, no matter where they have their baby. Previously, women who gave birth at home would receive £22, and those in hospital, £16.

Sunday 22 — **"Gift from Mr X"** An anonymous payment of £250,000 has been given to the National Gallery to help buy one of the world's finest art treasures, 'Les Grandes Baigneuses', a painting by the French artist Cezanne.

Monday 23 — **"Drilling Rig Order"** The Atlantic Refinery Company, based in Texas, has been awarded a three-year contract for oil-gas exploration to start when a platform drilling rig being made in Scotland at the John Brown shipyard is ready.

Tuesday 24 — **"7% Shock"** In Mr Wilson's bid to peg the home loan rates, the bank rate was increased from 5% to 7%. It is hoped to be a 'short term measure'.

HERE IN BRITAIN

"Stylish Shoes Bad For Children"

The British Medical Association is to ask the Government to control the type of footwear worn in schools following a survey showing that 715,000 schoolchildren aged five were examined and over 11% were suffering from a displaced big toe, while of the 780,900 aged 15 examined, 56% had the same deformity.

A consultant orthopaedic surgeon said the deformities were 'largely preventable' and he blamed shoes that were too small. Fashion - which it was stated had 'crept down as far as the toddler stage' - came in for much criticism, especially the Italian-style for boys.

AROUND THE WORLD

"Simple Monument for JFK"

President Kennedy's grave will be decorated with a *'classically simple'* monument that blends in with the contours of the grassy slope of the Arlington National Cemetery where he was buried nearly a year ago. The eternal flame, lit by Mrs Kennedy last year, will be the centrepiece to the monument which contains no enclosures, no tall vertical elements, and no statuary.

A seven-foot headstone engraved with the Presidential Seal, is being built into the hillside. The designer has stated that he wished to inject a feeling of *'serenity, tranquillity and rest'* to the former President's grave.

RULE OF THREE DRINKS

the new law on drinking and driving

the facts you should know

After a large degree of support for the campaign, the Minister for Transport has launched a further initiative stating the 'rule of three' when determining the drink drive limit. Whilst in an ideal world, there would be no drinking and driving, he said the Ministry can appreciate that this is not realistic, and instead, based on the advice from Glasgow University, they have published campaigns stating that no more than three single shots must be consumed before driving. This equates roughly to three single whiskies, three half-pints of beer, or a third of a bottle of wine. The Minister has defended certain posters being displayed across the country, which, in some cases depict crashed and mangled cars with bodies under the wheels, amidst criticism from The British Safety Council, who have called the posters *'tragically useless.'*

In the meantime, the Road Research Laboratory is continuing with their investigations into the correlation between fatal road traffic accidents and alcohol consumption and any changes in government legislation, and thus the law, hinges on the outcome of their report, due to be published at the beginning of next year. Their work involves investigations into fatal crashes, coupled with analysis of voluntary random breath tests on both drivers and pedestrians.

The campaign has amassed a large degree of support from, amongst others, The Royal Society for the Prevention of Accidents, local councils, some motoring organisations and even the brewers, who understand the ethos of the campaign is not 'anti-drink' and are cooperating by putting posters inside public houses and generally helping to raise awareness. The Minister has placed his emphasis on the main goal being to change social attitudes to drink driving using science and logic.

Nov 25th - Dec 1st 1964

IN THE NEWS

Wednesday 25 — **"Woman Customs Commissioner"** For the first time ever, a woman has been appointed Commissioner for Customs and Excise. She will receive congratulations from the Chancellor when she takes up her first duties.

Thursday 26 — **"Trafalgar Christmas Tree"** The Christmas tree for Trafalgar Square has been felled ready to be shipped from Norway next week. The tree is 63ft tall.

Friday 27 — **"Ships Collide"** 19 people are feared dead after a collision between an Israeli luxury liner and a Norwegian tanker in heavy fog just 40 miles off the coast of New York.

Saturday 28 — **"Hovercraft Before Tunnel"** A hovercraft ferry service between Dover and Calais is likely to start before the work on the Channel Tunnel begins. The service is being trialled to the Isle of Wight and, depending on the results, will be rolled out to France.

Sunday 29 — **"Outpatients Long Wait"** The Ministry of Health has released yet another memorandum asking hospitals to reduce the delays of out-patient's appointments after reports of *'substantial unnecessary waiting time for patients.'*

Monday 30 — **"Happy Birthday Mr Churchill"** Former Prime Minister Winston Churchill celebrated his 90th birthday at his home in Hyde Park Gate surrounded by his family. Mr Churchill will be receiving a 120lb birthday cake measuring 2ft in diameter and 8 inches deep, decorated with a large golden rose.

Tuesday 1 Dec — **"Mariner Finds its Star"** The US space probe Mariner IV has successfully found and fixed its gaze on its guiding star which will lead it on course for Mars in just a few days' time. The journey will take 8 months travelling at over 7,400 mph.

HERE IN BRITAIN

"Barking Deer"

Birmingham officials from the Royal Society for the Prevention of Cruelty to Animals are on the lookout for a small deer looking like creature that can *'run like a greyhound, jump like a small kangaroo and bark like a dog'.*

Many wildlife enthusiasts speculate that the creature may be a muntjac, but all are in agreement that it should not be roaming the Birmingham suburbs. The muntjac was first imported in the early 1900s and although rare to spot, there are estimated to be a few hundred living in the Warwickshire area.

AROUND THE WORLD

"Winston Churchill Day"

US President Johnson has taken the highly unusual decision to proclaim a 'Winston Churchill Day' as a tribute to the British wartime Prime Minister on his 90th Birthday. After being granted honorary US citizenship in 1963, Mr Churchill has become a respected and well-loved figure across America, where he toured giving lectures at universities just a few years after the end of the war.

President Johnson officially marked the day in the American calendar with a ceremonial tribute to the statesman and a plea to the American people to *'celebrate accordingly'.*

SECRET LIFE OF HAMILTON

One of America's founding fathers, Alexander Hamilton, a man who has been made immortal in the eyes of the American people, easily as beloved as President George Washington himself, finds himself caught up in a scandal decades after his death, after being accused of lying to President Washington and negotiating with a British spy unsanctioned. The allegations come from distinguished historian Julien Boyd, who is the editor of the Jefferson Papers, in a book titled 'Number 7'. British spy George Beckwith used to number his American informants to maintain confidentiality. What Boyd had previously believed to be information relayed to Beckwith from Number 1 on his informant list, turns out to have actually came from Hamilton.

Boyd describes how Hamilton was not concerned with personal gain, but instead was making secret attempts to control American foreign policy and was also conducting relations with Britain through unofficial channels; furthermore, Boyd has discovered that not only did Hamilton converse with Beckwith, but he then lied to President Washington about his dealings. By 1790, then Secretary of the Treasury, Hamilton, wanted to resume normal relations with the British, but due to British difficulty, this was not looked upon favourably by the young American government. Thus, Hamilton 'misrepresented' the view of the Americans to Beckwith in order to try and convince the British to be more forthcoming, which in turn forced him to misrepresent his dealings with Beckwith to the President. From there grew a web of lies and deceit which inevitably undermined the glorious figure he was seen as by the American media and public. Boyd later points out that Beckwith himself was serving his own agenda, as he was not only a spy for Britain, but was also part of a spy ring under the control of the Governor of Canada.

DEC 2ND - 8TH 1964

IN THE NEWS

Wednesday 2   **"Rocket Race to Mars"** Russia's new space rocket was reported by Western reports as *'hurtling'* into space in an attempt to reach Mars. The launch comes just days after that of U.S. Mariner IV, which is now over 500,000 miles away from earth towards the planet.

Thursday 3   **"Common Cold Research Unit"** The Common Cold Research Unit in Salisbury has developed a vaccine that could protect people from one strain out of the 50 known 'common cold' variants.

Friday 4   **"All Mini Team for Mote Carlo"** BMC have entered an all-mini contingent for the upcoming Monte Carlo Rally. The team is making their first reconnaissance journey of the 2,500-mile route.

Saturday 5   **"Helicopter Moves 32 Ton Crane"** The first operation of its kind in Britain saw a helicopter successfully remove a 32-ton crane, in several journeys, from the top of a recently completed 25 storeys building in Southampton.

Sunday 6   **"300 Seal Deaths"** In spite of numerous protests and petitions, the culling of over 300 female grey seals was carried out on the Farne Islands, just off the Northumberland Coast. The seals were shot at a rate of one per minute.

Monday 7   **"Tensions Brewing"** Argentina has brought her claim to the British administered Falkland Islands (Islas Malvinas) before the United Nations General Assembly. The Argentinian Foreign Minister claims the British 'illegally' took the island in 1833.

Tuesday 8   **"Go to the Chemist Instead"** Is the suggestion by the Office of Health Economics to try and help reduce unnecessary visits to the doctor or hospital. Pharmacists are extremely well qualified to give solutions for minor ailments.

HERE IN BRITAIN

"Beverly Sisters Blackout"

A television performance by the Beverly Sisters on ATV's 'Sunday Night at the London Palladium' left nothing to chance as the girls were dressed up in woolly black vests for the broadcast, instead of their intended costume – ordinary bras under see-through lacy tops.

The outfit change came after the 'Bev's' distracted the band and were drowned out by shrieks of wolf whistles at the full-dress rehearsal the previous night. The clothes were thought inappropriate, and the wardrobe mistress was sent out immediately to find some 'cover up' alternative clothing, the black vests.

AROUND THE WORLD

"Magnetic North Pole"

The Department of Mines and Technical Surveys are preoccupied with constantly tracking the position and movement of the magnetic North Pole. Since its discovery in 1904, the Pole has moved over 200 miles, mainly north-westerly from its original location, and recording these movements is vital to update maps for air and sea travel across the world.

Incidents of ships and aircraft using outdated maps and ending up off course are becoming more frequent. In 1962 it was estimated that the Pole was moving about 5 miles north and one mile east a year.

THE TRAFALGAR TREE

Norway's annual gift of a Christmas tree is in pride of place at Trafalgar Square. The 63-foot, four ton, tree, is one of the most impressive yet, and thousands of people flocked to London on Thursday to watch the Norwegian Ambassador ceremoniously switch the tree lights on. London's Regent Street and Oxford Street Christmas illuminations were switched on last week.

The first tree was sent from Oslo in 1947 as a token of gratitude to the British people for their help during the second world war when Great Britain was Norway's closest ally. London was where the Norwegian King Haakon VII and his government fled as their country was occupied, and it was from here that much of Norway's resistance movement was organised. Both the BBC and its Norwegian counterpart NRK would broadcast in Norwegian from London, something that was both an important source of information and a boost of morale for those who remained in Norway, where people would listen in secret to their forbidden radios. The idea to send a pine to Britain was first conceived by the Norwegian naval commando, Mons Urangsvå, who sent a tree from the island of Hisøy which had been cut down during a raid to London in 1942 as a gift to King Haakon and King George V decided that it should be installed in Trafalgar Square where it stood *'evergreen with defiant hope'*.

The trees come from the snow-covered forest area surrounding Oslo, known as "Oslomarka", an area populated with moose, lynx, roe deer, and even the odd wolf, and legions of pine trees. A worthy tree is located by the head forester and space is cleared around it to allow light from all angles, and it is tended through the years to secure optimal growth.

Dec 9th - 15th 1964

IN THE NEWS

Wednesday 9 — **"Steel Lifeboat Success"** After 4,500 miles of sea trials, a steel lifeboat acquired from the U.S. coastguard has proved to be extremely effective, and The Royal National Lifeboat Institution is likely to be commissioning several of its type to be built in Britain.

Thursday 10 — **"Nobel Prize Winner"** On the anniversary of the death of Alfred Nobel, Dr Martin Luther King became the 64th man to receive the Nobel Peace Prize. It was awarded for his outstanding humanitarian contribution to the race wars in America.

Friday 11 — **"World's Busiest Train line"** One new signal box has replaced the 22 previously required to deal with 'the world's busiest train line', between Euston to Crewe. Operators have likened the new automated system to *'playing chess with trains as pieces.'*

Saturday 12 — **"The Kenyan Republic"** Kenya became a republic within the Commonwealth at midnight last night when President Kenyatta's standard was hauled to the masthead at a stadium ceremony near the capital.

Sunday 13 — **"Law of Sunday Observance"** Religious authorities have supported the relaxation of many previously prohibited activities on a Sunday. These included amateur sports and cinema openings. Professional sport is, however, still restricted.

Monday 14 — **"Welsh Floods"** Over 700 British troops are on standby with amphibious vehicles to help deal with further flooding expected across mid and north Wales.

Tuesday 15 — **"Save the Grammar Schools"** Over 70 Conservative backbench MPs have launched a campaign to prevent the Labour government's plans for a change in status of grammar schools. Mr Douglas-Home has promised to raise the issue in Parliament.

HERE IN BRITAIN
"Well Nigh Perfect"

An 80-year-old Edinburgh man pleaded guilty to counterfeiting over 14,000 2-shilling (10p) pieces, born out of his resistance to seeking National Assistance. The money was described as 'well-nigh perfect' and given high praise by the chief assayer at the Royal Mint, who said that specimens sent to him for evaluation, *'are of excellent quality produced by an expert craftsman'.*

The man had been deceiving the banks and shops for over six years and was caught by accident when police were attending another matter in his building. He was sentenced to prison for two years.

AROUND THE WORLD
"Gods to go Hungry"

After the introduction of rationing in Kerela, India, because of severe wheat and grain shortages, even the Temples have been issued with ration cards. It is the practice in over 1,000 temples to make daily offerings to the deity of cooked rice which is later distributed among the temple employees and selected devotees.

Temple authorities are asking for a bigger ration on the ground that the present allocation is not enough for customary temple rituals and *'for meeting distribution commitments.'* The situation in the province is now being helped by the Indian Government.

Signs Of The Times

The Traffic Signs Committee propose that Britain's system of traffic signs should be replaced by a Continental-styled one, using mainly symbols instead of words. *"We believe",* the committee say, *"that our existing traffic signs are seriously out-of-date in relation to the present and foreseeable numbers and speeds of vehicles".* For the ordinary motorist the most important advance under the committee's proposals will be towards clarity and away from the reading or interpretation of words and letters of varying type. The committee say that 'Halt' and 'Slow' signs should be replaced by 'Stop' and 'Give Way' - the 'Give Way' sign being mandatory and to be used on all minor roads at junctions with primary routes in rural areas.

The old signs and their new replacements

Among the new signs, 'Turn Right', 'Turn Left', and 'Keep Left' would be indicated by white arrows on blue discs. For 'No Right', 'No Left', or 'No U-turn', the committee recommend the Continental red-and-black cancelled symbol signs. 'No Entry' would be shown by a white bar on a red disc, 'No Overtaking' by the Continental two-car silhouette with a cancelled symbol and one-way traffic by a simple system of arrows.

Since half the fatal or serious accidents occur at or near junctions, the committee say that minor and major roads should be very clearly distinguished by new, emphatic carriageway markings at the mouths of minor roads - a transverse, double broken white line half-way across and a longitudinal white warning line down the centre of 'the minor road'.

Dec 16th - 22nd 1964

IN THE NEWS

Wednesday 16   **"Statement of Intent"** The Government, TUC and employers have joined together to sign a 'Statement of Intent on Productivity, Prices and Incomes". Mr. Brown, Chancellor of the Exchequer said" *History is being made here today* ".

Thursday 17   **"Commemorative Postage Stamps"** the Postmaster General has revised the policy on commemorative stamps, saying that from now on there will only be new stamps to celebrate important national events, highlight British contribution to international affairs, and for the encouragement of 'minuscule' art.

Friday 18   **"Canadian Rule Britannia"** Conservatives in the Canadian Houses of Parliament erupted into chorus of 'Rule Britannia' after the House ruled to fly the Union Jack to demonstrate their commitment to the Commonwealth and allegiance to the Crown.

Saturday 19   **"Total Eclipse of the Moon"** A lunar eclipse occurred in the early hours of the morning, as the moon entered the shadow of the earth and was not therefore directly lit by the sun. The moon glowed a reddish blue between 12am and 4am.

Sunday 20   **"Free Prescriptions"** The Government announced that the NHS will be returning to free prescriptions in February next year, ending the 2s (10p) charge implemented in 1961.

Monday 21   **"End of Rail Fare Concessions"** Outdated concessionary fares on the railways for classes such as 'grooms with horses, drovers, conveyors with pigeons, racehorse attendants and regimental bands visiting tournaments', are to be withdrawn.

Tuesday 22   **"Drink Driving Clamp Down"** 1964 is likely to be the last year when only voluntary measures are placed on drink driving. The Ministry of Transport is taking heed from other European countries who have already implemented legal regulations.

HERE IN BRITAIN

"Abolition of the Death Penalty"

The abolition of the death penalty for all murders has come in a victorious fashion after a vote in the House of Commons, led by Mr Sydney Silverman, was passed with a majority of 185. Abolitionists cheered loudly following their victory and Mr Silverman was surrounded by a ring of admirers who shook his band and slapped him on the back.

The emotionally charged debate had lasted over seven hours. The two most recent executions took place in August this year and the abolition is likely to be confirmed before the end of next year.

AROUND THE WORLD

"Too Much Lean"

The Italian Government has met to consider calling upon international projects to help save the Leaning Tower of Pisa from collapse. The 800-year-old tower leans almost 16 feet off centre and there is an increased risk that it will fall.

The Soviets have pledged support, and the chairman of a Moscow commission discussed methods used to save buildings similarly threatened in Russia. *'In some cases, sandbags or cement were used in a cavity dug beneath foundations'*, he said, *'and hydraulic jacks were used to straighten the walls.*

WRIGHT BROTHERS 61ST

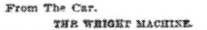

The first flight of the Wright Flyer, December 17, 1903, Orville piloting, Wilbur at the wingtip.

This month, celebrations were held to commemorate the sixty-first anniversary of the first flight by the Wright brothers at Kitty Hawk. The original machine is now displayed at the Smithsonian Institute having been formally presented to the United States by a nephew of the Wright's in 1948. Before then it was on show for 20 years at the British National Museum. In 1928, Orville Wright wrote of the decision to send it to London "because of the hostile and unfair attitude shown towards us by the officials of the Smithsonian Institute."

Each year since 1928 the flight has been commemorated on the slopes of Kill Devil Hill near the village of Kitty Hawk, North Carolina, where the Wright memorial stands. This austere column of granite has a circular staircase inside, and from the summit there is an uninterrupted view to the north and the scene of the Wrights' triumph. In 1903 it was a stretch of windswept sand and dunes, but now it is covered with thick grass, reeds, and bushes. Wreaths were laid at the foot of the memorial, 'Taps' sounded, and a procession made its way down the hill to the site of the Wrights' workshop and living quarters, now reconstructed. Close to them are the stone and marking posts of the first attempts at powered flight.

The first attempt to fly the aircraft made 61 years ago, because of a mishandling mishap at the start, failed. Four poles show the successful initial flights made on December 17 1903. The first, under the control of Orville Wright, covered 100ft in 12 seconds, the second, under Wilbur Wright, made 175ft. Orville covered 200ft on the third attempt and the final flight of the day was 852ft with a duration of 59 seconds.

Dec 23rd - 31st 1964

IN THE NEWS

Wednesday 23 — **"Tunes by Telephone"** The 'top-of-the-pops-by-telephone' service in Hull has become so popular that the Post Office stopped the service at peak times.

Thursday 24 — **"Dr Beeching to Retire"** The chairman of the British Railways Board is to retire and not be in charge of the survey into the integration of the British Transport System.

Friday 25 — **"Queen's Christmas Message"** Her Majesty's traditional message was televised and addressed the important role of the Commonwealth.

Saturday 26 — **"Driving Back from Christmas"** The Christmas traffic on Britain's roads was the busiest ever, setting new records as motorists struggled to get home.

Sunday 27 — **"Snowed In"** A giant blizzard swept across Britain causing over 3 million TV's to blackout over thirty counties.

Monday 28 — **"West Meets East"** Over 250,000 West Berliners have made the crossing into East Germany since Christmas eve to spend time with loved ones over Christmas.

Tuesday 29 — **"Clydebank Contract"** John Brown's shipyard will build the new liner to replace the Queen Mary, providing employment for several thousand men for about four years.

Wednesday 30 — **"Haircut Discrimination"** A scruffy appearance and Beetle-esque 'mop-head' haircuts, has deemed some Liverpool school leavers as *unacceptable for the workplace* by many potential employers.

Thursday 31 — **"World Speed Record"** Donald Campbell has set the world speed record across water at Dumbleyung Lake in Australia, reaching a speed of 276.33 mph.

HERE IN BRITAIN

"Cheap Christmas Travel"

Over 5,700 people, travelling on the £10 assisted passage programme, will make the journey from England to Australia on Christmas Day. A statement by the Australian Minister for Immigration announced that these Britons, all but 200 of whom will be travelling by sea, will be supported to relocate in the country. This final trip of the year will bring the total number of British migrants to Australia to 65,000, an increase over the 47,000 last year and the highest number recorded since the programme began at the end of the Second World War.

AROUND THE WORLD

"Indian Cyclone"

India and Ceylon have been hit by devastating floods and cyclones that have wrecked homes and towns in the South of the country. Over 200 million rupees worth of damage has been reported, with at least 350 people unaccounted for from the cyclone that hit Ceylon. The devastation caused by the disaster has been recorded as the worst in living memory. Over 1,500 bodies have been washed up on newly formed shores and thousands of acres of crops have been destroyed and schools, hospitals and homes flattened. The exact number of dead will never be known.

TURKEY FOR THE HOMELESS

A sea of long-haired men and grey beards could be seen gathered outside Westminster's Central Hall as Big Ben chimed noon, all of whom were waiting for Miss Betty Baxter, 'The Silver Lady', to serve up portion after portion of Christmas dinner. The event is now well known throughout Britain and homeless men make the journey, some from many miles away, for the occasion. One man this year, a former builder, came all the way from Lancaster. Adhering to the tradition of 'ladies first' meant that the minority of women present led the way into the hall where a mobile all-night cafeteria had been set up. Old fashioned café music was playing, and menus decorated the tables *'like Christmas cards',* as television cameras lined the walls to capture the festive event.

Miss Violet Elizabeth (Betty) Baxter, or as she is better known amongst tramps, 'The Silver Lady', has organised the annual Christmas dinner for the homeless since the 1930s. She runs a mobile cafeteria on London's embankment, and her name comes from the silver she gives out to homeless people to pay for a bed for the night and this year was no different, the Silver Lady gave out half crowns to all and socks to the men and gloves to the women.

The Charity itself was formed in 1880, by the Reverend Michael Paget Baxter, who was the proprietor of the Christian Herald newspaper and initially provided sustenance to people suffering from hunger, quickly growing to making gifts of clothing and accommodation for stranded women and girls. Miss Baxter, the founder's granddaughter, is still a director of the newspaper. Part of the funding for the Charity comes from the paper's donations and the rest from independent subscribers to the 'Silver Lady Fund'.

1964 Calendar

	January					
S	M	T	W	T	F	S
			1	2	3	4
5	6	7	8	9	10	11
12	13	14	15	16	17	18
19	20	21	22	23	24	25
26	27	28	29	30	31	

	February					
S	M	T	W	T	F	S
						1
2	3	4	5	6	7	8
9	10	11	12	13	14	15
16	17	18	19	20	21	22
23	24	25	26	27	28	29

	March					
S	M	T	W	T	F	S
1	2	3	4	5	6	7
8	9	10	11	12	13	14
15	16	17	18	19	20	21
22	23	24	25	26	27	28
29	30	31				

	April					
S	M	T	W	T	F	S
			1	2	3	4
5	6	7	8	9	10	11
12	13	14	15	16	17	18
19	20	21	22	23	24	25
26	27	28	29	30		

	May					
S	M	T	W	T	F	S
					1	2
3	4	5	6	7	8	9
10	11	12	13	14	15	16
17	18	19	20	21	22	23
24	25	26	27	28	29	30
31						

	June					
S	M	T	W	T	F	S
	1	2	3	4	5	6
7	8	9	10	11	12	13
14	15	16	17	18	19	20
21	22	23	24	25	26	27
28	29	30				

	July					
S	M	T	W	T	F	S
			1	2	3	4
5	6	7	8	9	10	11
12	13	14	15	16	17	18
19	20	21	22	23	24	25
26	27	28	29	30	31	

	August					
S	M	T	W	T	F	S
						1
2	3	4	5	6	7	8
9	10	11	12	13	14	15
16	17	18	19	20	21	22
23	24	25	26	27	28	29
30	31					

	September					
S	M	T	W	T	F	S
		1	2	3	4	5
6	7	8	9	10	11	12
13	14	15	16	17	18	19
20	21	22	23	24	25	26
27	28	29	30			

	October					
S	M	T	W	T	F	S
				1	2	3
4	5	6	7	8	9	10
11	12	13	14	15	16	17
18	19	20	21	22	23	24
25	26	27	28	29	30	31

	November					
S	M	T	W	T	F	S
1	2	3	4	5	6	7
8	9	10	11	12	13	14
15	16	17	18	19	20	21
22	23	24	25	26	27	28
29	30					

	December					
S	M	T	W	T	F	S
		1	2	3	4	5
6	7	8	9	10	11	12
13	14	15	16	17	18	19
20	21	22	23	24	25	26
27	28	29	30	31		

IF YOU ENJOYED THIS BOOK PLEASE LEAVE A RATING OR REVIEW AT AMAZON

Printed in Great Britain
by Amazon

2eef6525-920e-4ec1-aa49-0486b220e759R01